TOMORROW WILL BE TOO LATE

With Love and Gratitude
to the Members of My Eucharistic Community
in the Province of Saint Anne
and to
the Members of My Family
Who Taught Me the Values of Community
Lucien & Irene
and
Doris, Girard, Maurice, Pauline

TOMORROW WILL BE TOO LATE

A Life of Saint Peter Julian Eymard
Apostle of The Eucharist

NORMAN B. PELLETIER, SSS

ST PAULS

Alba House

Library of Congress Cataloging-in-Publication Data

Pelletier, Norman B.
    Tomorrow will be too late: a life of Saint Peter Julian Eymard, Apostle of the
Eucharist / Norman B. Pelletier.
      p. cm.
Originally published: Cleveland, Ohio : Emmanuel Pub., c1992.
    ISBN: 0-8189-0912-9 (alk. paper)
    1. Eymard, Pierre Julien, Saint, 1811-1868. 2. Christian saints—France—
Biography.   I. Title.

BX4700.E9 P45 2002
271'.79—dc21
[B]   2001045994

Produced and designed in the United States of America by the
Fathers and Brothers of the Society of St. Paul,
2187 Victory Boulevard, Staten Island, New York 10314-6603,
as part of their communications apostolate.

ISBN: 0-8189-0912-9

Printing Information:

Current Printing - first digit   1   2   3   4   5   6   7   8   9   10

Year of Current Printing - first year shown

2002   2003   2004   2005   2006   2007   2008   2009   2010

Contents

Foreword

One cannot speak of Saint Peter Julian Eymard without immediately calling attention to the love of his life, Jesus in the Eucharist. Peter Julian's personal journey towards the realization of his conviction that this extraordinary mystery of the Eucharist deserved a religious community to promote its worship and to proclaim its social and ecclesial implications did not come without a price. The costliest perhaps was his decision to leave the Society of Mary, the Marists, in whose religious family he had lived and labored for seventeen years. But, as he often repeated to his friends, it was Mary that led him to her Son in the Eucharist.

Peter Julian Eymard's spiritual journey was one of constant reevaluation and of new beginnings. At first he was attracted to the notion of reparation and saw that prayer before the Eucharist offered an opportunity to pray for the sins of mankind. This was an understandable reaction to the lingering social evils which the French Revolution in its initial excesses brought to his country. However, slowly he became aware of the further dimensions of this great mystery. He no longer desired to limit the Eucharist to the single dimension of reparation. Soon he began to proclaim the Eucharist in all of its remarkable richness.

Prayer and contemplation were the hallmarks of his spiritual search, and yet he described himself as being similar to the roving prophet, Jacob. Indeed, his apostolic life was as vigorous as his prayer life was intense. Always, whether preaching or praying, Peter Julian was focused on the mystery of the Eucharist, the bread of life. Mass and holy communion were the central events of the Christian life. He reminded his followers that eucharistic ministry was to be a preparation for these events and eucharistic prayer a consequence.

Today Saint Peter Julian Eymard remains an imposing figure in the Church as a model of eucharistic spirituality. He lived a life of deep prayerfulness yet he was also sensitive to the social implications of his eucharistic vocation. His prophetic insistence that the Eucharist is as much for sinners as it is for the upright, moved Pope John XXIII to call Peter Julian Eymard the "Apostle of the Eucharist" on the occasion of his canonization. This timely event occurred shortly after the first session of the Vatican Council where the Council's declaration about the Liturgy had just been issued.

The author of this Life of Saint Peter Julian Eymard, Father Norman B. Pelletier, SSS, was Superior General of the Congregation of the Blessed Sacrament and thus had ready access to the archives of the Congregation in Rome. It also gave Father Pelletier the opportunity to consult with others who have been researching the life and times of Saint Peter Julian Eymard. Father Pelletier has used his sources well, giving us a highly readable and inspiring life of Saint Peter Julian Eymard. He has captured the spirit of Saint Peter Julian and has provided his readers with a feeling for the man and his struggle throughout his spiritual quest. Father Pelletier invites us along a spiritual journey with Saint Peter Julian. It is a journey that has more than just historical relevance; it invites us to see the transformative power of the Eucharist in the life of someone captivated by this mystery of love.

Eugene LaVerdiere, SSS

Introduction

The novelist Morris L. West claimed that he had no taste for edifying stories because they often contained more fiction than his novels; and that he mistrusted "reported miracles." He further asserted that a holy person is someone who has managed by the end of his life to conform his character to that of Christ. Conformity with the Christ pattern, he declared, is never complete; it is never achieved without wounds and scars. The life of the saint is a sign of contradiction.

These words have served as a guide in the telling of the story of Saint Peter Julian Eymard, whose life, if not filled with contradictions, is at times enigmatic and reveals an elusive personality "scarred" by failures and disappointments but also full of courageous new beginnings.

This biography of Saint Peter Julian Eymard is intended for the general reader. Its aim is to provide an overview of the life and mission of a man who has often been called the "apostle of the Eucharist." He established the Congregation of the Blessed Sacrament, a group of religious men whose purpose is to promote the importance of the Eucharist for Christian living; he was also the founder of a women's Congregation, the Sister Servants of the Blessed Sacrament, with the same purpose. In the twentieth century a lay institute, Servitium Christi, was organized to share this Eucharistic spirituality.

I hope the telling of this story will give the reader an appreciation of the man Eymard, and of his mission; of how he was doggedly determined, in spite of hardships, setbacks, and poor health, to respond to that inner voice which beckoned him time and again to leave everything behind and to launch ahead into uncharted waters. God walked with him and taught him how to journey from a spiritual life oriented towards discipline, mortification, and personal effort to a way that was no less demanding but one whose focus was on God rather than the self. It was the way of love. "We must begin with love and then to virtue by way of the love of God, rather than take the negative aspects of our miseries as our point of departure. This way is easier, shorter and more passionate."

For Saint Peter Julian Eymard the love of God was disclosed and made available in the holy Eucharist and this insight formed the basis of his spirituality. He perceived how the Eucharist needed to become formative for Christian discipleship; indeed, the Second Vatican Council reminded the Church that this holy Mystery was formative of the Christian community itself, as an assembly of worship but also as a Church of service. Saint Peter Julian proclaimed, perhaps more by his life than by his writings (of which we have mostly personal letters to friends, relatives and colleagues), the power of the Eucharist for the renewal of Church and Society. In fact, he summoned people to a revolution. He said, "I want a revolution in the spiritual life… a revolution in the pulpit. We commit a big mistake in the spiritual life; we place too much emphasis on the negative. It's just the opposite. We have bled people enough. People need nourishment."

I have attempted to describe the journey of a man who lived in a cultural, social and political context totally different from our own. The political history of France in the nineteenth century is at times confusing but always complex. Saint Peter Julian lived in the aftermath of the French Revolution.

The battle of Waterloo in 1815 ended Napoleon Bonaparte's expansionist dream and brought the royal family back to the throne in France but the action precipitated the July Revolution of 1830. Then the February Revolution followed in 1848 which brought about the Second Republic from 1848 to 1852, and then the Second Empire was formed from 1852 to 1870 with Napoleon III.

Political and social upheavals were not limited to France during the nineteenth century. Italy, struggling towards national unity, was facing serious opposition from the Papal States and from other kingdoms in various parts of the country. It was also the time of the great famine in Ireland when countless numbers of Irish men, women and families migrated to America and Australia, while thousands stayed home and many died of starvation. In Britain, the Oxford Movement was in full swing and John Henry Newman was converted and entered the Catholic Church in 1845. In the United States after the death of its first and only elected bishop, John Carroll of Baltimore in 1815, a rash of anti-Catholic feeling resulted in the burning of churches in Boston and Philadelphia in 1834 and 1844; then the country experienced a terrible Civil War from 1861 to 1865. During this same period India saw the dissolution of the East India Company and became part of the British Empire.

It was a transitional moment in history in which European nation states struggled to fashion geographic and political identities. Few succeeded to do so peacefully, in fact, the alliance of throne and altar came apart with enduring traumatic consequences.

Every age has its crisis whether political, social, or religious but each one also produces significant personalities in the midst of turmoil and transition. The nineteenth century Church in France seemed overly fertile as it was richly blessed with remarkable people many of whom founded religious communities. The nineteenth century witnessed the establishment of the Oblates of Mary Immaculate by Bishop de Mazenod; the Sisters of the Good Shepherd by Mary Euphrasia Pelletier; the Religious of the Sacred Heart of Jesus by Madeleine Sophie Barat; the Society of Mary (Marists) by Jean Claude Marie Colin and that of the Institute of the Marist Brothers by St. Marcellin Champagnat; the Little Sisters of the Poor by Jeanne Jugan, to name but a few.

Peter Julian Eymard takes his place among the saints and founders of the Church's "oldest daughter," as France was called for centuries. This brief biography is a tribute to the spirit of Saint Peter Julian Eymard in the hope that the Eucharist which fascinated him and inspired his life may stimulate our own faithful response to God's constant, at times gentle and powerful invitation to love and service.

This account of the spiritual journey of Saint Peter Julian Eymard in no way claims to be comprehensive nor the last word on the subject. That task is left to more competent pens. Much of the material found in these pages has been drawn quite freely from two previous biographies written in French, one by Fr. George Troussier, SSS and the other by Msgr. Francis Trochu, as well as on Peter Julian Eymard's extensive correspondence to members of his two Congregations, to his many lay friends, and to his sisters.

To date the most scholarly work on the early years of Father Eymard and his Congregation has been done by Fr. Donald Cave, SSS. His spiritual journey has been recorded by the insightful work of Fr. Herve Thibault, SSS; and Fr. Laureat Saint-Pierre, SSS courageously pushed forward the frontiers of Eymard studies. An exhaustive "Life" of Saint Peter Julian was published in French by Fr. André Guitton, SSS. In Italy, Fr. Manuel Barbiero, SSS has written a remarkable thesis on Eymard. I am grateful to them for their contribution towards making Saint Peter Julian Eymard better known and for having made my task easier.

A personal word of thanks goes to Robyn Johnson, RSM whose skillful editing has resulted in greater clarity of thought and style; and to Fr. Donald Cave who painstakingly made certain that I never wandered too far from historical accuracy. A token of gratitude must also be given to everyone who has encouraged this work, especially those who saw a need for telling Saint Peter Julian Eymard's story in a straightforward narrative style for the general public.

Part One

"I wish to do something great
for the glory of God
and for the salvation
of my brethren"

Saint Peter Julian Eymard
September, 1854

Original parish church of La Mure

CHAPTER ONE

Always On
The Move

The commissioner of police shouted to the bystanders to behave and not to make trouble. For a brief moment the protesters calmed down but soon, like a wave slowly increasing in strength and power before breaking onto the shore, their voices exploded into a single refrain: "Don't take our saint away!"

The townspeople and faithful of the village of La Mure, nestled in the foothills of the French Alps, were loudly objecting to the removal of the body of Father Eymard from the local church cemetery. That the demonstration did not in fact turn more violent was due principally to the presence of the commissioner of police. He had been given orders by the mayor to maintain public order at all costs. The government Prefect himself had clearly indicated that armed guards would intervene if necessary to prevent civil disorder at the authorized removal of the remains of the founder of the Blessed Sacrament Congregation.

The opposition to the removal of the body had been led by the mayor's secretary upon the encouragement of Father Eymard's adopted sister, the only remaining "relative." She had left La Mure not to have to witness this painful incident.

The disciples of Father Eymard, upon the death of his sister Marianne, had petitioned the authorities to have his body transferred to Paris where the Congregation had just constructed a special place for it in the new chapel of their motherhouse.

As soon as the villagers of La Mure were notified of the request a public outcry arose in indignation. Almost as one voice they decried the "theft" of "their saint." Father Eymard was born and raised in La Mure. He returned frequently to visit his sisters and to offer Mass in the village church where he had been baptized. The residents of La Mure knew him personally. Many had attended his burial near the front gate of the church cemetery where the workers were now digging to remove the heavy lead box containing the oak coffin with the remains of "their saint."

They were determined not to give him up without a fight regardless of the mayor's promise to keep the transfer as peaceful as possible. The clamor of the housewives, children, and ordinary workmen began the moment the first shovel touched the earth at four that afternoon and continued like a Greek chorus until the casket was escorted out of town three hours later. The date was June 27, 1877, less than ten years after Father Eymard died.

He had traveled to La Mure from Paris via Vichy and Lyons unaware of the gravity of his illness. His own priestly and religious vocation had been the result of a long spiritual journey. His apostolic zeal had him sailing several times to Rome to obtain approval of his newly founded religious Congregation; and by coaches and trains to establish Cenacles, centers of Eucharistic devotion, in various parts of France; traveling continually to preach about the love of God manifested in the Blessed Sacrament. Even death had not kept him still. More important, however, was the spiritual journey of this French priest, which is the subject of this story. It is a testament to a man who left a legacy of spiritual values based on his fidelity to God's will. God pursued him even within the contentment of his ardent priestly commitment and the securities of his religious life as a Marist.

The outcry of the simple villagers of La Mure attested to the affection with which he was held as well as to the holiness which they attributed to him. It was this same fondness for their beloved founder that had prompted the Congregation of the Blessed Sacrament to retrieve the body of their "spiritual father."

Stone at the site of Fr. Eymard's first burial site, La Mure

Rue de Breuil, La Mure

CHAPTER TWO

The Journey Is Imagined

"It cost me dearly."

GROWING UP IN LA MURE

Peter Julian Eymard was born in 1811 in the village of La Mure, France. He was the only surviving child of his father's second marriage to Marie-Madeleine Pelorce. His stepsister Marianne, herself the only child to live to adulthood from the first marriage, lived with them. The parents subsequently adopted another daughter Nanette.

Peter Julian's father was a hardworking individual and a devout Christian. In addition to his regular church duties he had enrolled himself in a Eucharistic association whose orientation was rigorously penitential. In fact, religious life in France at this time was still breathing the stuffy air of Jansenism, a religious movement which presented religion in a very harsh and narrowly penitential manner by placing excessive emphasis on the role of sin and suffering, pain and sacrifice in Christian life.

This approach to religion had a strong appeal among very many good but unsophisticated believers. Peter Julian's father nourished his faith on this kind of spirituality. He personally had suffered so much from the loss of his first wife and six children from that marriage as well as from the death of the first three children from his second wife before Julian was born. These harsh realities did not leave his father unaffected or unscarred.

Peter Julian's father was never rich but he managed to eke out a respectable living by ingenuity and hard work. When he started a new life in La Mure with Marie-Madeleine Pelorce he struggled to make ends meet by sharpening knives, scissors, and a variety of tools. Soon he had earned enough money to rent space for his work in a building on Du Breuil Street. Some time later he bought the building next door where he established a small but profitable oil press. He did well enough to be able to hire someone to assist him. The oil was made from pressing walnuts under a huge grind stone being rotated by a donkey. It was a decent livelihood and it earned enough to support his family: a wife, a daughter, an adopted girl, and his last child, Julian, upon whom he had placed his hopes for the future of the family.

Growing up in La Mure was exciting for young Peter Julian. La Mure was then, as it remains today, the most important town of the area due to its location and its commerce. When Peter Julian ran about the streets of this truly picturesque hamlet, snugly embraced by a majestic range of alpine mountains, it already claimed a bustling population of about 1500 inhabitants.

His father had a small business and so there were many customers to attend to; and since he helped in the shop and did the deliveries of oil to his father's clients young Peter Julian developed a number of healthy social skills. The Eymard house included living quarters upstairs and working space on the ground floor. The building was situated on the main street of La Mure. Very little happened outside that passed unnoticed by this inquisitive child. Du Breuil street was always busy. It was the major road that connected the town of Gap in the south to the larger city of Grenoble to the north.

NAPOLEON MARCHES THROUGH TOWN

Great excitement stirred La Mure one day in March 1815 when Napoleon himself marched up Du Breuil street on his way to Paris with his faithful grenadiers. He had just escaped from the isle of Elba. Peter Julian was four years old then and stood by waving as the great general passed by. Impressionable as he was he never forgot the colorful plumage which some of the officers had been wearing that day. Later he would play soldier with his friends and had his sister make him something that resembled a feather for his cap.

One day he spotted a real feather at a nearby shop and couldn't resist it. He grabbed it and ran home to put it on his cap. He would surely be the best looking little soldier in La Mure, well at least the best dressed soldier among his friends which obviously was very important to him. He had been teased often enough by them of smelling like oil. Now he could proudly show them his new acquisition. See if they laugh at him now; he had a real feather for his cap. But the excitement didn't last. His joy turned to fear as soon as he got home. He didn't even have time to put the plume on his hat to see how great it would have looked. Remorse gripped him instantly and he rushed back to the shop as quickly as he could to return the stolen merchandise. He was sorry and upset with himself for having been so impulsive. He remained to some extent impulsive all his life.

Peter Julian assisted as an altar server at the local parish as did many boys his age. It was the custom at La Mure for the altar server to go up and down the main streets and ring a bell reminding worshipers that it was time for church. Every altar boy competed to be the one to ring the bell. It was a privilege besides being fun; after all you were the one announcing to the entire village that something quite special was about to happen. Not being timid but rather clever Peter Julian figured out that he could always get to ring the bell for the morning Mass and outmaneuver the other boys if he could get there first. But why rush and get up early in the morning when it was much easier to take the bell the night before. That's just what he did. He would on occasion take the bell home with him. In that way he reduced the competition without too much fuss.

Like his parents and sisters Peter Julian was devout and faithful to his church obligations. His mother and sisters had taken him to services when he was still very young. As soon as he could manage on his own he would often be seen entering the church for a quick visit to the Blessed Sacrament and for a short prayer to Our Lady. Many times he interrupted his daily chores and his deliveries of oil to perform his little religious exercises. He had a special place for his oil jug when he came to church. He would hide it behind the holy water font, in that way he could grab it quickly on his way out and the oil smell wouldn't offend anyone who might happen to be in church at the same time.

SEEDS OF A VOCATION

Sometimes he would play at being a priest. When the girls from the neighborhood came to the shop he would let them taste the walnut paste only if they promised to be his congregation and join him for prayers. Then he would don a ragged piece of cloth that served as a surplice and put a cross around his neck. They did notice, however, that he did more preaching than praying when he had an audience. Already Peter Julian was practicing a skill which he was later to exercise with great efficacy. No one at home failed to notice these early stirrings of a promising priestly vocation.

The austere Jansenist approach to the sacraments prevented children from receiving the holy Eucharist. So, in order to prepare for this great moment Peter Julian and a friend left their homes early one winter, amidst an early morning snow, so that they could reach a neighboring village church where, being unknown, they could attend Mass and hopefully go to confession. As it happened they got to the church well in time to serve Mass and so impressed the priest with their devotion that he agreed to hear their confession. The parish priest at La Mure would never have consented to their request for confession. He thought them too young and not sufficiently prepared for such a holy sacrament. This was a common residue of Jansenist thinking. Only on rare occasions could even the most devout receive the Eucharist. It made little sense to prepare for the sacrament if you would not be allowed to receive it. In any case, the two boys outwitted the local priest and made their first confession in spite of local custom. Many years later as a devout priest and successful preacher he would insist, "You take Communion to become holy, not because you already are."

The day finally came for him to make his first Communion. It was Passion Sunday. The date was March 16, 1823 and Peter Julian had passed his twelfth birthday. He had watched the adults at home make sacrifices during Lent and he had observed how they had fasted from food before going to Communion. He was not to do any less to prepare himself well for this important day. Once, while there was still snow on the ground he climbed barefoot to the top of the little hill behind his home to say a prayer at what is still today called Calvary hill because of the three crosses planted there on a small knoll overlooking the town.

His next ascetical venture proved less successful. He wanted to go without food in imitation of the Lenten fast of the most devout. He had planned to give his breakfast to the poor and himself go without. His sister caught him one morning as he was about to perform his secret charity. Needless to point out, that practice ended abruptly. Finally, the day arrived and Peter Julian made his first Holy Communion. It was a moment he would never forget. He had prepared so long and so seriously for this. Thirty years later he told a friend, "What wonderful graces God gave me that day!"

Peter Julian attended the local school and did quite well in his studies. He was not a brilliant student but he was intelligent and worked hard to achieve success. No sooner had he turned thirteen than his father decided to take him out of school. By now, his father reasoned, his son had acquired more skills in mathematics and in writing than he would ever need to maintain and continue the small family business. The boy was crushed. Neither his mother nor the parish priest dared intervene on his behalf. Mr. Eymard was firm and determined. The boy could not understand his father's behavior. He had spoken to him earlier about wanting to become a priest. At that time his father had refused to discuss it. But now having made his Holy Communion Peter Julian hoped that his father would appreciate the genuineness of his attraction to the priesthood. He was puzzled and confused by his father's refusal and with his latest decision to keep him from continuing his schooling. He wondered whether it was something he had done wrong or was it that his father expected more of him in school? Had he not performed his chores responsibly?

PILGRIMAGE

Upset and discouraged at seeing the vocation upon which he had set his dreams slowly vanishing by his father's latest decree, he set out on a pilgrimage to the shrine of Notre Dame du Laus (Our Lady of the Lake) some thirty miles away. Somehow he got permission to go. He headed south following the flow of the river Drac through the village of Corps; and then before reaching the city of Gap he quit the river's dependable lead and pushed southeastward until he spotted the shrine some ten kilometers beyond the town of Gap. When he finally reached the shrine he immediately entered the church to pour his heart out at the feet of Our Lady.

Notre Dame du Laus had become a popular Marian shrine soon after Our Lady had appeared to a young peasant girl in the latter part of the seventeenth century. A short time before the Oblates of Mary Immaculate had been given the religious administration of the shrine. On this particular day a certain Oblate missionary, Fr. Touche, happened to be in the church at the moment our young pilgrim approached the altar of Our Lady. No sooner had this thirteen year old finished telling Mary the story that was breaking his heart than the seasoned missionary called him over. Fr. Touche was a most respected preacher in the area.

Still anxious about his own role in his father's refusal to allow him to pursue a religious vocation, Peter Julian persuaded the priest to hear his general confession; which he did. Then the boy broke down and told him everything. Fr. Touche was not a man to be easily impressed, but there was something about this boy. His sincerity, his innocence, his genuine piety, whatever it was that this Oblate priest saw it was enough to convince him that the boy should not give up his quest. "But my father will not give me permission," Peter Julian insisted. "There are no buts about it, you will have to start learning Latin. Besides, I think you should receive Communion each Sunday." And thus started a lifelong friendship. It was also the beginning of another friendship, one that really had begun earlier at La Mure but which now took solid root in Peter Julian. It was to the Blessed Virgin Mary to whom he had turned in his pain and confusion. She had heard and answered him. This devotion grew and deepened over the years. Our Lady would play a significant role not only in Peter Julian's initial vocation but throughout all of his life.

Peter Julian returned home happy and more convinced than ever that he should pursue his dream of becoming a priest some day; however, he never fully understood the reasons for his father's refusal. This young thirteen year old could not be expected to appreciate the concerns of a parent who had placed his hopes for the future material welfare of the family on his only son. As far as Peter Julian was concerned the biggest obstacle was still there, his father's steadfast refusal. Yet for the time being he could keep his father satisfied by doing his chores well. With this approach he was convinced his father would have no cause to complain and much less suspect what he had plotted to do. During his rounds about town Peter Julian had met some boys who were studying Latin at the small local college. From one of them he learned what he would need to start studying Latin. With his mother's encouragement he purchased a secondhand Latin grammar.

For more than two years the young man struggled to learn Latin in secret. During the summer holidays he would take advantage of the presence of visiting seminarians to have them look at his work and to correct his exercises. Otherwise he was quite on his own. Only his mother and his father's employee knew what he was up to. As soon as his father left the shop Peter Julian would pull out his Latin grammar and do some exercises or memorize conjugations and declensions. The hired man never betrayed him to his father.

He found it very taxing to be both attentive to his chores and devoted to his Latin studies. Such behavior for a thirteen year old required enormous strength of character, determination and a high level of sustained motivation. Without any apparent and immediate positive reinforcements Peter Julian remained faithful until the day he thought opportune to approach his father and confess what he had been doing for the last couple of years. One day he asked the big question. "College? It's much too expensive!" his father shouted. Peter Julian knew instantly that it was pointless to argue with his father particularly when it involved spending hard-earned money. It was useless to even think of debating the issue. There would be no money for education.

This latest rebuff notwithstanding, Peter Julian remained steadfast. He was not about to dismiss two years of concentrated effort in learning Latin without a struggle. Nor was he ready to consider adjusting his vocational sights elsewhere than on the priesthood.

After all, he was his father's son. The strength of character which Mr. Eymard demonstrated by establishing himself as a respectable small businessman, having started with practically nothing when he first arrived in La Mure, was not lost on his son. Peter Julian showed himself as single-minded and as resourceful as his father. By now he was almost sixteen years old and fast becoming an independent young man. He took his father's outburst as a challenge.

SCHOOL

Peter Julian took it upon himself to inquire from among some friends who were close to the mayor of La Mure on how he could obtain one of the three scholarships available to the poor of the town. He applied and was given a scholarship. But going to school on a scholarship intended for the indigent was not appreciated by the school principal. "They own a family business and they are not in any way needy," was the way the principal reacted to the news. Somewhat disadvantaged scholastically when he started classes Peter Julian studied very hard and soon caught up to his classmates. In a short time he even surpassed many of them.

The school principal was not in the least supportive. As a matter of fact he was so upset that Peter Julian was attending his school on a scholarship intended for students who were poor that he made every effort to remind Peter Julian of that fact. Not once did he let him forget that he was not paying his own way but that he was at school at someone else's expense. The memory of this experience never left him. Years later recalling these school days he acknowledged: "It cost me dearly. I was treated with contempt and often humiliated. The principal made me pay in so many ways for that education. He wouldn't allow me to recreate with the others. Instead he had me light his fireplace, sweep his office and his classroom, and had me do a hundred other chores. Thus I was daily reminded that I was one of the three 'poor' students."

Peter Julian was not the only one to suffer. His father could no longer endure the humiliation of being considered indigent. In a town like La Mure it soon became public knowledge that the son of a respected businessman was attending school at public expense. So one day Mr. Eymard marched up to the school to share his sentiments with the principal. "Well simply take him out of this school, if that's the way you feel!" shouted the principal. Once again Peter Julian found himself at the oil press in his father's shop. He took up his work in the oil shed and faithfully delivered the orders of oil to his father's customers as he had so often done before.

One day a priest came to La Mure to visit his own family. This visiting priest was looking for a young man to do odd jobs around his residence and his place of work. Peter Julian went to visit the priest and in no time at all he had him persuading his father to let him go to Grenoble under the supervision of this priest in return for room and board and some lessons in Latin. It must have been the sheer authority of the priest that finally convinced Mr. Eymard to let his son go because he surely preferred to have him by his side learning the oil business which he hoped one day Peter Julian would continue.

DISAPPOINTMENTS AND LOSSES

As it turned out the arrangement in Grenoble was not exactly what Peter Julian had been promised and surely nothing like he had anticipated. The "hospital" at which the priest was chaplain happened to be an insane asylum. Peter Julian had odd jobs to do but since this chaplaincy was only part of the many other duties the priest performed, he consequently had little or no time for those Latin lessons Peter Julian had looked forward to. As a result Peter Julian was left to his own ingenuity.

Once he had accomplished all his chores around the asylum he would study Latin on his own from books he acquired from the library. This schedule took up his interest for awhile but soon this seventeen year old became discouraged and felt quite lonely with no one with whom he could share his interests or even to correct his Latin exercises. The environment of the asylum did not help raise his spirits. He was not happy in that situation but the fact that he could continue to study Latin in preparation for the priesthood kept him going. He was determined to follow through on this quest so convinced was he that God was calling him to serve Him in this way. He was willing to sacrifice many small comforts and the company of friends to pursue this chosen path, a path which Fr. Touche had confirmed and encouraged some years before in the sanctuary of Our Lady of Laus. The memory of this event sustained him. Often he would recall it in prayer.

One day as Peter Julian was crossing the asylum courtyard the director, unaware that Peter Julian had not been alerted already, blurted out: "So young man, I hear your mother passed away!" Peter Julian was stunned. He couldn't believe what he had just heard. He had not been told; and the shock of hearing of his mother's death "in passing" left him numb, cold and bewildered. It was only once he had reached the chapel could he let go and cry until his pain was spent. Then he implored Our Lady to become his mother from this moment onward.

Peter Julian departed immediately for home. When he arrived the funeral was over and he never had a chance to say his good-byes. His father greeted him tearfully with the sadness of a man who had buried too many already. Peter Julian realized that it would now be harder than ever for his father to let him go. So once again Peter Julian took up his post alongside his father in the oil shed; and though they both mourned the same loss their grief was never shared. It remained personal. As for Peter Julian and his quest for the priesthood, everything had now come to a full stop. But in his heart he knew that the pursuit of his goal was merely postponed, not canceled.

Meanwhile life continued in the Eymard household as best it could with Peter Julian, his father, Marianne, and Nanette. As the months went by Mr. Eymard got accustomed to having his son by his side but if he thought that Peter Julian had reconciled himself to following in his father's footsteps he was sadly surprised when one night the Oblate priest, who had been preaching the Lenten retreat at the parish church, arrived at the house to request permission for Peter Julian to enter the Oblate novitiate. Mr. Eymard put up his best and last fight to keep his son near him, yet through it all he understood that this battle had waged too long and there was no way he could win. His son was now eighteen years old. He knew what he wanted. He always had. There would be no more resisting this obvious call from God. It was too persistent and more importantly too demanding to be simply the whim of an idealistic adolescent. He had not yet overcome the pain that had accompanied the death of his wife and God was asking him to give up his son. So be it.

After a brief visit to the shrine of Notre Dame du Laus, Peter Julian returned home to take leave of his father and sisters. On June 7, 1829, Peter Julian put on the religious habit of the Oblates of Mary at their novitiate house in Marseilles. He was very happy in Marseilles. He believed he had finally secured his way to the priesthood. It was not meant to be, however, as God had other plans.

No more than five months into his novitiate Peter Julian fell sick; first he complained of headaches and then of severe stomach pains. The local doctor, unable to diagnose his illness, bled him twice and then pronounced him incurable. Peter Julian was sent back home to die. He was bundled up in the middle of winter and put into a coach for the more than 250 kilometer ride to La Mure, the fare payable upon arrival.

He arrived in an exhausted and hopeless condition and was immediately bedridden. His father was distraught. Marianne and Nanette nursed him for months. Little by little his condition improved. It was during this time of convalescence that Peter Julian learned to play the violin which, years later during times of stress, he would play for relaxation. As Peter Julian's health grew stronger the Eymard household began to normalize. Slowly he began to get around on his own and to do things for himself. It was very probably out of this mothering experience when they had to nurse him daily, as he hovered between life and death, that Marianne and Nanette's overly protective instincts towards him took definite shape and against which he continually struggled to free himself.

One day his father suddenly fell seriously sick and his condition worsened rapidly. They watched helplessly as this once robust man weakened. His strength deteriorated daily. He died in Peter Julian's arms on March 3, 1831. He was 65 years old. Peter Julian, Marianne, and Nanette grieved their father's death as they had that of their mother less than two years earlier.

The home of Fr. Eymard as it appears today at 67 Rue du Breuil, La Mure

The pastoral setting of the church at Monteynard

CHAPTER THREE

The Journey Begins

"God calls me today, tomorrow will be too late."

SEMINARY AND PRIESTHOOD

With his father's death Peter Julian inherited the house and the family business, none of which interested him. His only interest, as it always had been, was to pursue his studies for the priesthood. So he left everything in the hands of his sister Marianne who was now 32 years old.

Peter Julian applied for acceptance to the diocesan seminary of Grenoble, possibly thinking that the diocesan schedule of studies would be less taxing on his fragile health than the rigors of a religious community. Because he had not followed a regular course of studies the seminary officials would consider his application only upon the recommendation of his local parish priest. What Peter Julian thought would be a simple and routine matter turned out to be a near disaster. When he went to the presbytery to request the priest's recommendation he was received very coolly and told that a letter of this nature required much thought and deliberation and that it would be delivered to the house in due time. Well, Peter Julian and his sister immediately concluded that the parish priest's recommendation might not be too complimentary if he needed that much time to evaluate a young man whose family he had known and whose parents he had just buried. When the letter arrived at the house it was quickly dispatched into the fireplace. Peter Julian would take his chances without it.

Placing his trust in God and in the Blessed Virgin, he left for Grenoble to seek entrance to the seminary there. Upon arriving in the city he visited the cathedral located near the seminary. During his prayer he wondered whether he had acted properly by destroying the letter of the parish priest and whether the seminary officials would even consider his application without a recommendation. His journey to the seminary had been long and arduous and filled with many disappointments. Would this be the final rejection? Was he now to be sent home on the next coach with his dream neatly packed under his arm? He would leave everything at the feet of Our Lady.

Anxious, yet always firm in his resolution, he left the cathedral. On the steps he came face to face with Bishop de Mazenod, the founder of the Oblates, who had received him at the novitiate in Marseilles two years earlier. He was amazed at seeing Peter Julian actually alive and in Grenoble. Peter Julian recounted all that happened since Marseilles and that he was now on his way to the diocesan seminary. "Come, I'm on my way there myself. Let me tell them all the bad things I know about you," Monsignor said with a grin. On Monsignor's word and recommendation Peter Julian was accepted into the seminary. In his heart Peter Julian knew that Mary had indeed been attentive to his prayer.

Peter Julian followed the regular course of theological studies offered at the Grenoble seminary along with the other seminarians pursuing the same goal. He did not distinguish himself for his academic accomplishments, but he worked hard and achieved average grades in his subjects. He seemed to have learned to pace himself and to control his excessive desire to excel. This zeal flowed naturally enough from this resolute and resourceful young man. At times, however, it may have contributed to the worsening of his already fragile physical condition with which he would have to struggle and suffer all his life. But at least during his seminary days he was able to balance his time for study with the time he needed to rest and thereby not ruin his prospects of ordination because of a recurrence of his past illness.

After three years of theological and spiritual training Peter Julian was ordained on Sunday, July 20, 1834 by the bishop of Grenoble, Bishop de Bruillard. The day after his ordination Peter Julian set out alone for the shrine of Notre Dame de L'Osier (Our Lady of the Willow) some 20 kilometers southwest of the city. The following day, Tuesday, he celebrated his first Mass at the altar of Our Lady. Why this shrine? One would have thought Peter Julian would have chosen to celebrate this momentous and long sought after event at his parish church or at Notre Dame du Laus where his journey to the priesthood had begun more than 10 years earlier at the feet of Mary and with the decisive encouragement of the Oblate missionary, Father Touche.

Apparently the Oblates featured prominently in Peter Julian's choice of Our Lady of L'Osier for his first Mass. This shrine was under the administration of the Oblates and the priest in charge was Peter Julian's former Novice Director from Marseilles who had recently been assigned here along with another Oblate priest who had been a novice with him. Peter Julian had decided to come to L'Osier not merely to rekindle past friendships or because of his devotion to this shrine of which we have no evidence of his fondness. He was hoping to be readmitted into the Oblate community and expected the encouragement of his friends in that community. He had not invited his sisters to accompany him doubtless because he felt he could not have resisted their pleas to remain with the diocese, and consequently under their mothering eye, had they known his plans to join the Oblates.

Weeks passed and he had not returned to La Mure. His sister Marianne knew him well enough to begin to suspect his intentions. So she wrote to the bishop about her concerns. On August 23, a month after his first Mass, Peter Julian received a letter from his bishop ordering him to go to La Mure for a short rest before being assigned to a parish in the diocese. The bishop was obviously acquiescing to the request of his sisters who were always solicitous of their brother's frail health.

However, the Oblate superiors were not inclined to encourage his readmission to their community. Consequently, Peter Julian returned to La Mure and awaited an assignment from the bishop. He accepted all of these events as being God's will for him and remained at home until October when the bishop wrote again requesting him to go to Chatte, a village not far from L'Osier, to assist the parish priest as his curate. Peter Julian arrived at his new assignment in time to celebrate Mass in the parish church on Sunday, October 26.

CHATTE AND MONTEYNARD

Chatte, a parish of about 2000 people, is situated south of Grenoble a short distance from the Isere river as it flows west on its journey to the Rhone. The parishioners were devout in the practice of their faith. Here Peter Julian, as a newly ordained priest, performed all of the duties expected of a parish curate. He preached, heard confessions, taught catechism, and celebrated Mass, often at the altar of Our Lady. Witnesses testified to his religious devotion and to the fact that he would spend a lot of time in the church praying before the tabernacle and composing his sermons there. When leading the stations of the cross he would become quite emotional. One time he even walked down from the pulpit without being able to finish the prayers.

Peter Julian's health remained precarious in Chatte. At times he was bedridden and would cough up blood. Because of his physical deterioration the pastor's sister and housekeeper was not eager to keep this invalid in the presbytery. She was afraid he had contracted tuberculosis, which is very probably what Peter Julian had struggled with in Marseilles and from which he nearly died afterwards in La Mure. She feared he would contaminate the bedroom he occupied. The pastor could not endure her constant nagging and was eventually pressured to resolve the situation. So after serving the parish for two and a half years he was reassigned by the bishop in July of 1837 as parish priest to a small church a short distance from La Mure. The bishop wrote:

> "The pastor of La Mure asks for your appointment to the parish of Monteynard. I am pleased to grant his request. My dear friend see if your health offers any obstacle. The climate is not cold like that of La Mure, and I suppose your sister will join you and attend to your health. If you accept this appointment, go right away and notify the pastor of Chatte that you will be replaced at once."

Peter Julian's sisters, always solicitous of their brother's delicate condition, had also been actively pulling strings with their parish priest to have the bishop reassign their brother nearer to them so they could keep a close eye on him.

Upon receiving the bishop's letter on July 2 he made arrangements to depart. He went home to La Mure and then he made a short retreat at Notre Dame du Laus before taking up his duties at Monteynard. He arrived there before the end of the month.

PARISH PRIEST

Peter Julian's arrival at Monteynard was greeted with enthusiasm. Less then a dozen kilometers north of La Mure, Monteynard is perched high upon a ridge with a spectacular view of the fertile valley below through which meanders the river Drac. At that time Monteynard counted about 450 parishioners and had had no resident priest for some time. The church had fallen into disrepair and the new parish priest dedicated his immediate energies for its restoration. He petitioned his friends from Grenoble to contribute to his new mission. With their help he was able to purchase new vestments for the liturgy as well as other church furnishings among which included a church bell. Through the generosity of the Carthusians of the Grand Chartreuse he was able to replace the main altar with one of gilded wood. For a small price he bought a statue of Our Lady from his former parish priest in La Mure. The parishioners were impressed. His sisters set up housekeeping at the presbytery having brought whatever was necessary from their own home.

As he had been in Chatte, Peter Julian continued to be extravagantly generous with his own money as well as with the grocery money his sisters thought to be safely hidden from him. They scolded him for giving away some of their personal clothing to itinerant beggars at the door. They often found the cupboard empty of the food they had set aside for the next meal.

He loved to visit the sick and to inquire about the nature of their illness. He had acquired a passing knowledge of the medicinal value of some of the local herbs and would teach those who were interested to recognize certain plants; he instructed them on how they should be prepared and when they ought to be used.

On one occasion he worked with a deaf-mute in order to prepare him for first Communion. His pastoral sensitivity led him to accommodate the men working during the day by inviting them to the presbytery in the evenings for confession. Some of them stayed till 9 or 10 o'clock. To relax from his heavy pastoral schedule he would play his violin. He was also known to indulge in a little snuff.

Once he helped a young unmarried couple living in a hovel by providing them with adequate housing. He also restored a small chapel on the northern end of the village so that people could attend services there instead of at the parish church which was at some distance from the center of town in the opposite direction. He would hold services in the chapel especially during Lent and for Marian devotions during May. The parishioners of Monteynard loved him and he was happy among them. A most interesting aspect of his parish ministry was the program he devised to catechize the children by telling them Bible stories which captured their imaginations and served also to introduce important religious lessons for the adults who accompanied the children.

Yet, hardly had he arrived at his new assignment than Fr. Touche, his old friend and confessor from Notre Dame du Laus, informed Peter Julian of the newly established religious community called the Society of Mary or Marists. That news was like flint to fire. His dream of joining a religious community, after two faulty starts with the Oblates, was again rekindled. He lost no time. He went to Lyons to speak with Fr. Colin, the Superior and Founder of the Marists. Upon returning to Monteynard he wrote to his bishop, Bishop de Bruillard, asking to be released from his diocesan obligations so that he could join this new missionary religious community. While awaiting the bishop's reply he sent a letter off to a friend, Fr. Dumolard. The letter is dated 4 October 1838.

> "Being now convinced of my vocation, it seems to me that nothing will stop me. Already I have twice made the sacrifice, without being able to carry it through. The third time I hope will be eternal. Even if I knew I would die on the way, how happy I would be! Even if I derived no other advantage from it than that enjoyed by your brother: to die in a religious house."

The bishop's reply arrived:

> "I believe my dear friend that the good Lord wants you in our diocesan missions under the patronage of St. Francis Regis. Busy yourself entirely in preparing your mind by study and your heart by prayer, humility, and detachment from the world for the important work from which God draws so much glory. Strengthen your health also. The missions require a great soul and robust health."

In so many words the bishop told him that if he wanted missionary work he could find it in the diocese. Meanwhile Fr. Colin wrote to him: "I approve your wish, consider yourself as if in the novitiate."

Now he found himself in a genuine quandary as to what to do. He had been accepted to join the Marists but his bishop would not release him. He did not want to appear obstinate towards his superior yet this attraction to religious life had returned unsolicited and with such vigor that he could not well ignore its pull. Meanwhile, Fr. Colin wrote again on 4 May, 1839:

"The opposition which God permits to arise, the more painful as it comes from so eminent a source, will strengthen your resolve.... Again, with due respect launch your attack on the bishop. God will hear you."

Before acting on this advice, being always resourceful, he prepared the ground by invoking the support of the vicar general to intervene on his behalf. Now Peter Julian was ready to confront his bishop. He wrote:

"Give the Society of Mary this poor priest as the first fruit of your diocese; he is no use to you and is as weak as a small reed. The Blessed Virgin will be pleased with this meager offering, insignificant as it is."

Bishop de Bruillard's reply came on July 4.

"The trial has lasted long enough. Enter upon the path God calls you, and there labor for your sanctification and that of others. I will take care of the matter of replacing you."

Meanwhile, thinking that her brother was set upon joining the diocesan mission project as the bishop had suggested, Marianne went to Grenoble to implore the bishop not to let this happen. The bishop explained that this was not the case at all. In fact, it was worse than she had imagined. While she was in Grenoble, Peter Julian was already getting ready to receive his replacement who was to arrive on Sunday evening, August 18. No one at Monteynard knew of his plans to leave. He arranged everything so that his departure would go unnoticed.

To avoid the painful scene his departure would surely occasion, he hired a musician to play at the entrance of the church after Sunday Mass in order to distract the people while he made his way out of town. He had profited from his sister's absence to prepare his bags and had them removed the night before. So after Mass he quickly went to the presbytery and left from there to catch the carriage which would bring him to Grenoble to pay a final visit to his bishop.

On the way to the carriage he met his sister and her friends who were, at that very moment, returning from Grenoble. She had heard the whole story from the bishop and there was nothing for her to do now but to plead with her brother to spend at least one more day with her. His wrenching reply to her pleas was, "Sister, God calls me today. Tomorrow will be too late." She fainted in the arms of her friends as he staggered away to catch his coach, anxious that should he turn to look back for even a glimpse he would not find the strength to go through with his decision. Years later, his friend Fr. Mayet recounted that the parting had been so agonizing for him that he had barely managed to climb into the coach.

The very next day he wrote to his sisters from Grenoble:

"The bishop advises me to set out from here so as not to renew your grief and not to witness the tears of my parishioners. You know my delicate feelings. I did not hide them from you, but if I returned to Monteynard I would either fall sick or I would risk the loss of my vocation. May God's holy will be done. And if death awaits me, both you and I will have the same merit. It was necessary for you to share my sacrifice as Mary shared that of Christ. God be praised. Now dry your tears...."

The parishioners of Monteynard put up a valiant fight to get their parish priest to return. They petitioned the bishop and even sent a delegation to Lyons to try to persuade Peter Julian to return to them.

They obtained the assurances of the bishop that if they could persuade Peter Julian to return with them to Monteynard he himself would formally attend his homecoming at the parish. They soon learned, however, that there was no chance of changing Peter Julian's mind.

They met him in Lyons at the novitiate house. Peter Julian was surprised to see them but deeply touched by their outpouring of affection and by their firm resolve to return to their parish with their parish priest. Their initiative on his behalf left him shaken and profoundly moved. Nevertheless, he tried to explain to them that it was God who had called him away and that he had to remain faithful to his vocation. He could not go back with them.

Disappointed and dejected they returned to Monteynard and attempted to explain to their fellow parishioners how God could seemingly be so cruel. They had had no priest for so long a time and then He sent them someone who cared for them and listened to them and absolved them. They had become attached to him. At that very moment God had literally snatched him from them. They were alone again, but not quite in the same way they had been before Peter Julian entered their lives, for he had demonstrated God's love and forgiveness during his ministry to them.

Basilica of N.D. de Fourvière, original church on the left

CHAPTER FOUR

The Journey Continues

"My life rushes and rages like water from a flood."

MARIST VOCATION: 1839-1855

On Tuesday the 20th of August 1839 Peter Julian began his novitiate training under the direction of Father Pierre Colin, the founder's elder brother. Eight days into his novitiate program he made the annual retreat with the forty members of the new Marist Community. A retreat preached by its founder, Jean-Claude Colin. In a letter to a priest friend he expressed the following sentiments, "I have been here two months and they have passed like two days. As soon as I arrived I felt satisfied. I was where I belonged." By the end of November, still a novice, Peter Julian was sent to the Marist College at Belley as spiritual director. The following February he pronounced his vows as a Marist and remained in formation work at the Belley College.

His abrupt departure from Monteynard did not leave his relationship with his sisters unaffected. They were understandably very hurt and could not make much sense of his behavior. Peter Julian tried to repair the emotional damage he had caused. He wrote to a friend, Fr. Brun, asking him to spend some time with them and try to console them. The hurt persisted. On September 6, two weeks into his novitiate, he wrote assuring them of his affection and telling them that his sacrifice in leaving them and the people of Monteynard was surely less then theirs. They remained unmoved by his pleas. For months they refused to answer his letters. In August of the following year he was still pleading with them to write to him and at the same time telling them of his decision not to visit them because of his fear of stirring anew the entire painful affair. Eventually and with time the wounds did begin to heal, but the scars would not easily or quickly disappear.

In the meantime Peter Julian attended to the duties of his new vocation and devoted himself to his life of prayer. In his spiritual notes we find this entry: "God has made me understand that I was not praying enough in my heart, that I reasoned too much; and that a safe means was to let myself be led like a child, to do simply the good that I knew, present and urgent, and nothing more." It was in prayer that he found the comfort he had sought from his sisters: "This morning… our Lord granted me a great favor during my thanksgiving after Mass. He firmly but lovingly reproached me saying, 'Are you afraid to attach yourself to Me, to leave with Me the care of your future?'" He had found the strength to continue.

Once more his health broke down as it had so often before. This time he became dangerously ill with a pulmonary condition. Fr. Colin came running to his bedside insisting that he not die because "it'll kill me too," he said. Neither of them were soon to die. Peter Julian recovered and Fr. Colin eventually outlived him.

PROVINCIAL

For relaxation Peter Julian would pick up his violin or sit at the piano and entertain the community with military tunes. In November of 1844 Fr. Colin promoted him to the office of Provincial Superior and with this appointment he had to quit the College and relocate in Lyons at the motherhouse called Puylata. His new job left him little time for the musical diversions he had grown accustomed to at the College. He undertook an enormous amount of work and complained that the days were too short: "As Provincial, I am in charge of our communities in France and abroad and for me the sun sets too early."

As Provincial he traveled north to Le Havre, on one occasion, to preside at the departure of thirteen Marist religious being assigned to missions in the Pacific. He expressed his intense desire to follow them:

> "How happy I would be to go to the foreign missions, even though I could accomplish so little there. At least I might offer to God the entire sacrifice of myself — country, relatives, friends, acquaintances, mother tongue — of everything I have learned and be obliged to begin over again.... What a glorious moment it is when, with one foot on land and the other in the boat, one is about to leave everything behind and to sacrifice everything, to give oneself to God alone. This is to die. This would fill me with joy to the brim."

His friend and fellow Marist, Fr. Mayet, noted how full of apostolic zeal he was for the missions; however, God never permitted him to follow this dream. His health would not have survived the rigors of life in the missions. With his poor health he could barely manage the winters in France. In fact, he pushed his delicate body too often to the limits. In this respect he did not need to consider the foreign missions for hardship and sacrifice. After serving as Provincial for two years Fr.

Colin moved him to the post of Visitor General. This position carried with it many new and demanding responsibilities.

During the next several years he traveled extensively to the Marist religious communities in France. He was also in constant demand as a Lenten preacher in the churches of the area. Apparently his administrative work did not cripple his apostolic zeal. He was known not only for his effective preaching but also for the way with which he ministered to people.

Once, while visiting a hospital, he came upon an old man who was constantly boasting about his acquaintance with Napoleon, having been a drummer in his army. The old man, apparently, was more intent on recounting his military adventures than his sins. Peter Julian struck up a conversation with him one day and was soon subjected to the old man's tale of his exploits as Napoleon's drummer. Listening intently, Peter Julian quickly remembered his own "exploits" with the drum at Belley College when he would march up and down the hallways beating his drum to entertain the boys and drive away their loneliness. "I'm a drummer, too," said Peter Julian to the old soldier. "Fancy that," the old man replied, "a drummer priest." "How many marches do you know?" asked the priest. "Fourteen," shot back the soldier. "Well, then you beat me. I only know ten," answered Peter Julian.

From there the two went on to share stories about the emperor with Peter Julian telling him how he had seen the emperor marching through La Mure on his return from exile. Then, tactfully, Peter Julian steered the conversation to Napoleon's final exile at St. Helena island and delicately recounted how the emperor was converted. With a tear streaking down the trenches of his aged face, the old soldier made his confession and, like his hero, he too converted.

Violence and civil unrest marked most of France during the revolution of 1848. In Lyons, social and political disturbances were deeply felt. The silk industry was hit hard with high unemployment and frequent shutdowns. Some religious communities in their concern to resolve part of the massive unemployment had set up silk workrooms where poor workers could earn a day's wage. The regular silk workers, however, perceived this effort as an attempt to undermine their jobs by providing cheap labor. They went on a rampage and destroyed the shops which had been set up in a number of religious convents. Riots broke out as economic chaos spread throughout the city.

Religious communities with their large houses and extensive properties became the target of the workers' frustration. The danger to religious persons was further aggravated by a decree of the Provisional Government in March of that year which outlawed all religious congregations. As a consequence of this action on the part of the new government, religious superiors closed their novitiates and vacated their convents. Their members were sent home or to local parishes until the trouble subsided.

At the motherhouse of the Marists a few priests decided to stay on. Among them was Peter Julian. One day while walking along the streets he came upon a band of rioters who, upon spotting him, shouted: "There's one of those priests. Let's throw him in the river." The crowd went wild with excitement, feeling it would get some satisfaction with this brazen gesture of contempt against a representative of a group they believed had betrayed them. They took hold of him but before their enthusiasm got the best of them someone from the crowd shouted: "That's Father Eymard!" Voices from the mob repeated: "No, No, not him! Father Eymard is a friend of the workers." There was a moment of hesitation; the shouting stopped. Father Eymard noticed their eyes focusing on him and slowly their heads nodded in recognition.

Without releasing him the crowd veered from the river and started its climb to the motherhouse, this time their jeers

turned into cheers. They escorted him back to his house singing "rebel" songs. As they deposited him on his doorstep they
guaranteed his safety and that of the other priests in the house
by hoisting the tricolor flag above the door of the house.

A few days later after recovering from the incident he
courageously took to the streets again, this time in search of
the mob which he found at the work yard and thanked them
for their protection. Father Eymard wrote to his sister about
the incident,

> "I hear that you were disturbed about the events in
> Lyons and about me, but rest assured that I was al-
> ways safe; I was never in danger. We were even
> given a guard at the front door, and we go out wear-
> ing our cassocks with no problem at all."

Father Eymard's physical condition continued to be a concern. His work frequently affected his health. He told his sisters: "I have no idea how time flies so quickly and every night
I wonder how I get anything done. My migraines have started
up again. It's been awhile since I have been bothered by them
and you know there's practically nothing to be done for migraines." During the struggles of 1848 it seems he incurred an
injury to his ear which was apparently caused by the noise of
an exploding cannon. Over the years the problem was aggravated and he eventually became totally deaf in that ear.

In the early months of 1849 his work brought him to Paris
for the first time. His business was at the Marist house there
but he took the occasion to visit the royal palace at Versailles
which, after the execution of Louis XVI, had been opened to
the public. Like many of the clergy, during and after the revolution, he remained a sympathetic royalist while at the same
time being distressed by the lot of the poor and the shocking
conditions of the working class. It was no surprise then to see

him kneeling in prayer on the spot where king Louis XVI was guillotined and to hear him afterward saying how sad he was that day and how he had prayed for the "saintly Louis XVI." It was also during this visit to Paris that he met for the first time Raymond de Cuers who would later share with him the birth pangs of the new Blessed Sacrament community. De Cuers had been in Paris with the pianist, and recent convert, Hermann Cohen, both of whom were involved with the Nocturnal Adoration Society, an organization whose purpose was to promote nighttime prayer in the presence of the Blessed Sacrament. Father Eymard was impressed by the practice and devotion to the Blessed Sacrament he witnessed in Paris.

The following year he was instrumental in obtaining the necessary permissions from the archdiocese in Lyons for a group of lay people who wanted to start a nocturnal adoration organization in that city. A year later he was again involved in inviting and in seeing Mother Dubouché's Third Order Reparation Sisters established in Lyons. On January 29, 1851 Father Eymard inaugurated the arrival in Lyons of this newly founded religious congregation dedicated to the Blessed Sacrament by celebrating Mass for them in their chapel.

FOURVIÈRE

It was just a few days before, on the 21st of January, that Father Eymard had a religious experience at the shrine of Our Lady of Fourvière in Lyons. From this moment he began to pursue an idea with which he had been preoccupied for some time: of establishing a group of men devoted to adoration of the Blessed Sacrament, just as Mother Dubouché had done for women. This project had been the subject of his prayer for a considerable time. He would outline his idea in a projected letter to Fr. Colin, dated February 3, 1851:

"After deep reflection, having prayed a great deal and having sought advice, I have at last resolved to open my heart to you about a thought which I have been resisting for a long time, which pursues me constantly, reproaching me with turning a deaf ear to the voice of God. It is this: one day at Fourvière (January 21) I was strongly affected by the thought of:...."

The letter continues to describe his profound concern for the growing needs of God's people and how the Eucharist could prove to be an effective response to these needs. His growing appreciation of the Eucharist along with his apostolic sensitivity led him to insist that the reasons for founding a group of men dedicated to the Eucharist was in response to the religious conditions he perceived as needing a solution: (1) The spiritual abandonment of secular priests; (2) The lack of spiritual direction for the laity; and (3) The lack of devotion towards the Blessed Sacrament as well as the offenses committed against it. This idea of establishing a Eucharistic group of men was largely motivated by apostolic concerns. Father Eymard saw the Eucharist as a means of fulfilling the spiritual needs of clergy and laity. He equally insisted the Blessed Sacrament be justly worshiped and become a powerful source for people's spiritual development.

THIRD ORDER OF MARY

Up until that time Father Eymard had been very active with the Third Order of Mary which Fr. Colin had given him the charge of. This was a group of lay people associated with the Marist Community who shared their spirituality. Father Eymard took his responsibility very seriously and as a consequence of his attention and his vision for the Third Order it grew to include separate groups for married men, single men, and one for young women. He devoted a large amount of his time to the spiritual development of each of these groups with several meetings a month.

He was so enthused about the spiritual progress of the members of the Third Order of Mary that he requested official approval from Rome for this group. Pope Pius IX granted official approbation for the Third Order. Eymard was understandably elated at the news but greatly embarrassed when he presented a *fait accompli* to Fr. Colin, the Superior General, who was furious at Eymard's "initiative" in procuring Papal approval without his knowledge or authorization. What often seemed to Father Eymard as mere initiative or simple enthusiasm was regularly interpreted as impulsive behavior by others. However, this time he had unquestionably overstepped the bounds of propriety. Consequently, the incident nearly destroyed his relationship with the Superior General.

Soon afterwards Father Eymard was relieved of his charge of the Third Order of Mary and assigned as Superior of the Marist College at La Seyne sur Mer. In the autumn of 1851 he left Lyons, leaving behind his many friends and his treasured members of the Third Order of Mary, and set out for the south of France.

LA SEYNE-SUR-MER

The College of Sainte Marie at La Seyne-Sur-Mer belonged to the local diocese, but the administration had been entrusted to the Marists. It was located on the Mediterranean coast within the region of the Côte d'Azur about halfway between Marseilles and St. Tropez. Immediately upon arriving at the College Father Eymard tackled his new assignment with the same energy and single-mindedness with which he had assumed his other responsibilities. This new assignment severely taxed his energies and talents because the school was in shambles and on the verge of closing; yet his zeal and enthusiasm sustained him. Of those days at the College he wrote:

> "My life is a continual immolation. From morning to night I am at everyone's disposal. There's a knock at my door each minute for a thousand different things. I can't for one second open a book, pick up my pen. I can't even get to do my spiritual reading. It's very hard on me.... Oh, it's very tempting to react in a curt and abrupt manner and to display a severe attitude; it would be easy to cut short and to distance oneself. But such behavior is neither good nor charitable."

His indefatigable dedication paid off. He was eventually able to set the school on a solid footing.

Soon after he arrived at La Seyne he was faced with a situation that tested his leadership. It happened as a direct result of the coup d'etat of December, 1851 which brought Louis Napoleon to power. Large segments of the population reacted with sporadic acts of violence in protest. The Toulon area where La Seyne was situated was not spared.

One night a large crowd gathered, and frustrated by their inability to cause trouble in Toulon due to a heavy military presence, turned their anger against the Marist College a short distance from the city. Warned of the impending assault to the College, Father Eymard let the students retire peacefully without telling them a word about the danger. He then invited the teachers to spend the night together in prayer before the Blessed Sacrament. Father Eymard himself described the incident to his sisters:

"People have alarmed you about our situation here. It is true that we ran great danger. I came near being massacred and burned along with the school of which I have charge. These monsters actually intended to bowl with the heads of our boys. One hour after midnight on December 7, two thousand men headed toward our school and were not more than a half hour away when, realizing that one of their leaders was absent, decided to postpone the affair until the following day. The next day we were saved. A frightened curate had come to alert me of their plots. The good God gave me confidence in His Providence and I remained steadfast. Our Toulon prisons and the forts are filled to overflowing with prisoners. Three days ago forty women, involved in the uprising, were brought to the prison. It is a horrible thing to see.... 2000 rebels have been arrested, at least so I am told.

"How good is God to have saved our district. Those who threatened were bad men. I am sort of their chaplain, at least for those on board the Genereux (a prison ship) whose captain is the father of one of our students. I go there on Sunday to say Mass, preach, and visit these poor wretches numbering about three hundred. We have given them medals. Some of them have changed and many are repentant. I walk through their midst and they gather around me and we talk. But alas, how sad it is to have to say to oneself: among these men are assassins, perjurers, men of blood. Their leaders and bosses are to blame for taking advantage of these ignorant and fiery people of the South."

His troubles were not over. In the Spring an epidemic of measles broke out at the school. Many were afflicted. The few who were spared, including himself, came down with influenza.

In a letter to Mrs. Jordan, whose friendship he cultivated while director of the Third Order in Lyons and who would remain his lifelong spiritual confidante, he described how life was like for him at the school. The letter is dated January 22, 1852:

"You want me to tell you about myself; my life rushes and rages like water from a flood with lots of noise and gushing. An educational institution involves so many events and occurrences. God be blessed! Daily I sacrifice my own needs.

"On the other hand, the climate is good, the sky beautiful, and the surrounding nature is rich and green reminding one of a perpetual Spring. I can't tell you much about the ways of the South; I hardly know them. God has blessed this region with generous souls. There are more reasons here, than in our region, to admire the power of grace; because these Southerners with their explosive nature and their lighthearted manner and tender hearts do become saints, and great ones at that. It is hard for us, coming from the north to appreciate them. But when God sends them our way He provides the grace."

For the next few years the College prospered under his able direction. The student enrolment increased and the College programs expanded. He did have to pay a price, however. The cost to his health was at times considerable. At one point he came down with pneumonia and was required by the doctor to remain bedridden. Another time his doctor ordered him to take some rest away from the school. His bout with pneumonia seemed to have resulted from an incident, recorded by Fr. Mayet:

> "One day Father Eymard was on his way by coach for some much needed rest at the country house of Mr. Mulsant, a then famous naturalist. The two men were quite fond of each other. Upon reaching a nearby town Fr. Eymard asked the coach driver to wait for him a few minutes. The driver said he would. No sooner was Eymard out of sight than the impertinent driver drove off. Father Eymard gave chase and had to run three miles to catch up with the coach which he was able to do while it was climbing a hill. When Eymard recounted the story some time later someone asked: What did you say to the driver? Nothing, I was just so happy to be back in the coach."

On another occasion, when recalling this same incident, he confessed: "I saw at once that I had foolishly risked my health. But what could I do about it? It was not my fault, and there was no other way to remedy the situation. Instead of being sad and upset I laughed with my fellow travelers as if nothing had happened; nevertheless, I contracted a serious illness because of it."

Although his work was demanding and his health precarious, he still found time for all sorts of other ministries. Towards the end of 1854, at the height of the Crimean War, French soldiers and sailors were garrisoned at La Seyne. Because of an outbreak of dysentery the 43rd Regiment had postponed its departure. Father Eymard did not lose any time in taking advantage of the situation. He invited the officers and the medical staff to dine at the College and was able to obtain permission to visit the troops. Daily for two weeks he visited the men, talking to them about their faith, and at times even applying some of his "home remedies." Towards the end of the bivouac he held a three day retreat and finished with about two hundred soldiers receiving Holy Communion, some for the first time.

Another time he helped in a local parish and became friendly with the pastor. Sadly and suddenly the pastor took sick, suffered a heart attack and died. Because of the great affection which the people had towards Father Eymard the bishop asked him to take charge of the parish until he could find a replacement. In his zeal and enthusiasm for the spiritual welfare of the people, but unmindful of his health, he accepted the bishop's offer. Not unexpectedly his health gave out. His headaches returned and he was on the brink of suffering a complete breakdown. Several times the doctor forced him to get away to the country for rest. In a letter dated April 25, 1855 he wrote to his Marist superior:

> "I keep going; now weak, then again a little better. My cough seems unwilling to quit. What can I do? Let it alone. I hope you are not forgetting the request to send someone to replace me. The end of the school year is close at hand and I am at the end of my strength, but satisfied that it will soon be over for me. I intend from time to time to go to Maubel, if that is possible. I trust that you will not take my request as a sign of discouragement. No. Here my confreres are such that it would truly be unfair for me to complain. They are all so kind and dedicated."

During the time Father Eymard was at the College, and for some time before, a Eucharistic thread was being delicately woven throughout the fabric of his spirituality. Now and then God would give him a glimpse of where He intended to lead him. In a series of letters to Marguerite Guillot, a friend and devout member of the Third Order of Mary, he revealed just how committed he had become to this Eucharistic attraction and to what lengths he was ready to go in order to pursue this divine invitation: "Let me tell you that I would not want to die without seeing realized a great and wonderful idea which God awakened in my heart concerning the worship of Jesus in the Blessed Sacrament." In a subsequent letter he elaborated on how this "great and wonderful idea" was unfolding beyond a mere private and personal devotion to "founding a Blessed Sacrament Order."

He described further how this "great idea" had taken hold of him one morning during his prayer of Thanksgiving after Mass.

> "I was suddenly seized by this strong feeling of gratitude and love for Jesus, and I said to Him: 'Is there not something great that I can do for you?' And a gentle, peaceful idea, yet powerful and clear, made me happy to be able to devote myself to the service of the Blessed Sacrament."

These spiritual insights would get stronger and become clearer during the next twelve to eighteen months. His attraction to the Eucharist intensified, but for a long time he thought it could all be integrated within his vocation as a Marist. What was actually happening, however, was the powerful pull of grace which would eventually lead him to quit, after great suffering, his Marist vocation. He struggled to deal with this new call from God with a lot of uncertainty and with much anguish.

Fr. Eymard as a Marist priest

CHAPTER FIVE

The End Of A
Journey

"God is urging me on."

"YOU ARE FIRST OF ALL A MARIST"

For seventeen years, from the time he joined the ranks of the Marist Community, Father Eymard enjoyed the reputation of being a responsible and self-sacrificing member of that Order. The Marists entrusted him with many important positions in their religious family. At various times he served as Novice Master, Provincial Superior, Visitor General, Superior of the College at La Seyne, and Director of the Third Order of Mary.

While he gave himself wholeheartedly to his Marist vocation, God was at the same time knocking at the door of his heart with another invitation. God was calling him to a Eucharistic vocation.

The origins of this Eucharistic inspiration are traced to two powerful religious experiences. The first occurred on May 25, 1845 while he carried the Blessed Sacrament in procession at the Church of St. Paul, in Lyons. During that Corpus Christi procession he was profoundly moved to focus his spiritual attention on the person of Christ and he resolved to concentrate his preaching on Christ in the Eucharist. The second took place on 21 January 1851 at the Shrine of Our Lady of Fourvière where he was powerfully motivated to establish a group of men dedicated to adoring Christ in the Eucharist in response to certain pastoral needs of the Church. Despite the fact that these special graces had marked him profoundly, Eymard nonetheless remained cautious and tentative about any plans to focus his Eucharistic inspiration in a concrete manner which would have required him to assume sole responsibility for this venture.

To some extent Father Eymard had received encouragement from the Founder of the Marists for his Eucharistic ministry especially during the last years at La Seyne and in Toulon where the Nocturnal Adoration Society was already functioning and where he regularly preached at Eucharistic devotions in St. Mary's Cathedral every Friday night to an ever increasing group of men and women from the Adoration Society.

In the meanwhile Father Eymard, during the period of his tenure as superior of the College community in La Seyne (1851-1855), was collaborating with De Cuers in the hopes of establishing the Order of the Blessed Sacrament. Although it was De Cuers who had taken the initiative to actually recruit people with the intention of forming an Order of priests devoted to perpetual adoration of the Eucharist, it was Eymard who was called upon to help promote the project by writing the first draft of a possible set of rules to guide the group. In fact, Eymard went so far as to actively encourage certain students within the Marist College to consider a Eucharistic vocation. Once it was discovered that the Marist superior of the College, namely Eymard, had been recruiting prospective Marist candidates for another type of vocation, Eymard's colleagues at the College were shocked and his superiors in Lyons sought to have him disciplined.

In June of 1855, his superior, Fr. Favre, announced that he would visit him at the College of La Seyne but in the meantime he should be advised that the Society of Mary could not encourage a Eucharistic project and furthermore Favre ordered him to terminate his involvement in this Eucharistic venture.

> "You are first of all a Marist; and the Society of Mary is the bark of your salvation. You should behave so prudently that not even a shadow of criticism can be leveled against you concerning this Eucharistic project which, in any case, should not be your concern as a dedicated Marist."

With these remarks Fr. Favre intended to curtail Father Eymard's participation in the Eucharistic project. Eymard was dismayed by this decision. He tried to argue his case but without success. He would not be permitted to pursue the establishment of a Eucharistic project while a member of the Marist Society.

Disheartened by this news, Eymard turned to prayer for strength and comfort. He realized for the first time that the stakes were going to be extremely high if he were to pursue the inspiration which he now strongly believed was from God. He was not sure how he would find his way through this dilemma. In the face of this opposition on the part of his superiors and of the personal turmoil which it was causing in him he seemed, remarkably, more determined than ever to remain faithful to this Eucharistic idea which was taking more definite shape in his soul. He shared his feelings with his friend Fr. Mayet:

> "God is urging me on. This thought of establishing the work of the Blessed Sacrament is an attraction for me; it is making me better. It is gentle, strong,

calm, and satisfying. I see all that it will cost me. No one establishes a new work without being crucified. I am giving up a secure situation and will be exposed to poverty, contempt and destitution. If the affair does not succeed, people will ridicule me. I see all this, I feel it all. But I seek only the will of God."

Rebuffed by his superiors but emboldened by his heightened awareness and eager responsiveness to what he perceived as God's will, he appealed to Rome.

Providentially, his old friend and spiritual adviser Fr. Touche happened to stop by La Seyne on his way to Marseilles to board a ship for Rome. Father Eymard opened his soul to him. Fr. Touche's advice followed: "Your project is the work of God, but it must be submitted to the head of the Church for testing." Consequently, Touche agreed to present personally to the Pope a petition Eymard had prepared. Touche sailed from the port of Marseilles on 12 August for the eternal city.

PETITION TO ROME

Subsequently, Father Eymard then left La Seyne for a much needed rest at the insistence of his doctor. From the thermal baths at Mount Doré he wrote: "This is a cold place. I have not met anyone I know. I am quite alone, as I wish to be. But heaven is overhead, and at my side is the tabernacle: I have all I need."

Some time later he wrote:

"The water treatment has been good for me. God, in His divine goodness, seems to have given this means of relief to me to ask of me greater devotedness in His service. Therefore, I wish to labor more and more for His glory and to win men's hearts for Him. How good God is, willing to make use of so poor and wretched a person. God does not need us. But, when He decides to use our wretchedness and nothingness for His glory, when He gives us the honor of suffering for His name, we are indeed blessed."

Fr. Touche arrived in Rome on August 27 and a few days later presented Eymard's written petition to the Holy Father. It read in part:

"Most Holy Father: Permit the least of your children, a priest of the Society of Mary, in utter simplicity, to lay at your feet the thought of his soul. As it is impossible for me to go to Rome at the present time, Fr. Touche consents to take my place and to be the interpreter of my feelings.

"For the past four years I have felt myself strongly urged by grace to ask my superior for permission to devote myself entirely to the glory and service of Our Lord Jesus Christ in the Eucharist. For three years I resisted this inner impulse, fearing that it might be merely a natural attraction or a deception of the devil. However, the fear of resisting God's voice made me open my mind to Fr. Alphonsus, Provincial of the Capuchins, and now Assistant General in Rome. He advised me to test this idea even further and, if it persisted, to lay the matter before my Superior General. This I did. The very Rev. Father Colin, after hearing me, gave me this reply: 'I believe the idea which you have so long experienced comes from God and will procure His greater glory. Some day you will be able to carry it out.'

"Holy Father, [...] this powerful and gentle thought entered my mind: Why should not the greatest mystery have its own religious Order as have the other mysteries; why should there not be men with a perpetual mission of prayer at the feet of Christ in His Divine Sacrament? [...]

"The Society of the Blessed Sacrament would not confine itself to the mission of prayer and contemplation. It would in an apostolic way devote itself to the salvation of souls by employing every means inspired by prudent, enlightened zeal and the divine charity of Jesus Christ. It would labor to bring to the feet of Jesus in the Eucharist the greatest possible number of adorers by forming societies of adorers in the world.

Then Eymard explains how this Eucharistic apostolate could develop. The letter continues.

"Already six priests and six students of philosophy earnestly desire to vow themselves to this Eucharistic idea....

"There remains the personal question regarding myself. Very Rev. Father Favre, Father Colin's successor, with regard to my idea and the encouragement given to me by his predecessor, is unwilling to favor it outside the Marist Society, nor will he grant me permission to labor in its behalf, saying that he has no power to do so and referring me to your Holiness' decision. It seems to me Holy Father that giving to Jesus a poor child of Mary does not take away anything from the glory of His Blessed Mother. During the sixteen years that I have been a religious, I have held the offices of Provincial and assistant General. I am now relieved of all these duties and my withdrawal can nowise harm the Society of Mary.

Holy Father, my case is in your hands."

The letter was signed: Peter Eymard, Marist priest, and dated, August 2, 1855.

The Pope blessed and encouraged the project but noted that necessary permissions needed to be obtained from the Superior General and the local bishop in order to proceed.

Fr. Favre and his Consultors, on the other hand, did not see things in quite the same way. On the contrary, they again rejected his plan for a Eucharistic project. Favre felt strongly that a Eucharistic orientation was incompatible with the aims of the Marists. The Marist superior feared the damage this venture might cause to the young Marist Congregation; he was perhaps also saddened by the eventual loss of a competent, holy, and respected member of the Society. Father Eymard had never refused an assignment and had been often called upon to assume a number of responsible and at times most demanding tasks in the Marist community. Now, however, the message was different but no less demanding. Either drop the idea of a Eucharistic project or quit the Marists.

By the end of September Fr. Eymard had been relieved of his post as the superior of the College at La Seyne and was sent away for a period of rest at Chaintre, now the novitiate of the Marists. He wrote to Fr. Touche: "Here I am, I do not venture to say on Calvary, for I am not worthy of that, but in a state of trial, in a position of complete dependence on God alone. Please pray for me."

Fr. Eymard obediently dropped every direct contact relating to the Eucharistic project, nevertheless he remained firmly convinced that his Eucharistic inspiration was a sure invitation from the Lord. But how could he proceed without the approval of his superiors? The year 1855 came to a close with him agonizing over this predicament.

"FOR ME ROME IS THE POPE"

No resolution seemed forthcoming until one day in February Fr. Favre informed Eymard that he had to journey to Rome on business and that he would be willing to discuss the matter with the Holy Father.

> "I will present your affair to the Pope, and I hope you will submit to whatever the Pope says."
> "Absolutely, and with all my heart," replied Eymard.

He knew that Pius IX had already blessed the project and would surely not go back on his word. The Eucharistic project seemed secure.

Fr. Favre left for Rome at the end of February. Father Eymard wrote from Chaintré: "I suffer and I hope." He compared himself to someone at sea "who has only a plank to cling to and who abandons himself to the mercy of the wind with full trust in the goodness of God." "At Chaintré I prayed. I may even say that never have I prayed and suffered so much, begging God to make known His holy will."

It wasn't until April 22 that Fr. Favre, having returned from Rome, finally came to see him. It was nine in the morning and Fr. Favre asked him to walk with him in the garden so they could talk. They were still at Chaintré. Favre broke the news. This is how Eymard recalls the event shortly after it took place:

"Rome," he said, "is of the opinion that I not grant you permission to leave to undertake this Eucharistic project."

"Very well, Father," replied Father Eymard without hesitation, "the matter is settled."

The whole agonizing affair lasted but a few brief moments. Rome had spoken and he would submit. He would recommit himself to his Marist vocation and definitively drop his involvement with the Eucharistic project. All of a sudden, it all seemed so simple. So quickly everything had been settled. Both men were relieved.

The two of them continued to walk and they talked about how Eymard could resume his work. After certain arrangements had been agreed upon, Fr. Favre began to share his impressions about Rome and his visit with the Holy Father. Father Eymard, curious to know precisely what the Pope had said about the Eucharistic project, asked Favre to tell him how it had all happened.

Fr. Favre replied:

"I saw your friends and advisors, Fr. Alphonsus, and bishop Luquet, and Fr. Jandel, the Master General of the Dominicans, and all of them told me that I should not release you from the Marists and furthermore that you should not be allowed to continue working for a Eucharistic venture."

"And how did the Pope put it to you?" asked Father Eymard.

The Superior General hesitated, visibly embarrassed, and haltingly confessed:

"When I found myself in the presence of the Pope I was so moved that I forgot to mention your situation altogether." He added, "This was no doubt permitted by God."

Father Eymard stared at him in shock. He could hardly believe what he had just heard, but he fully comprehended the implications of Fr. Favre's avowal. The Holy Father had not rejected his proposal. That was clear to him, and critical for the whole affair.

"Well then," exclaimed Father Eymard, "nothing at all has been settled. For me Rome is the Pope."

"In that case," Favre shot back, "you must leave the Marists. I cannot and must not free you from your vows."

Father Eymard was stunned by his superior's reaction, and when he regained his composure he requested whether he would allow him to work at the Eucharistic project for a few years until it was well on its feet. Fr. Favre refused outright. There would be no compromise on the issue of the Eucharistic venture.

"God has been drawing me powerfully to this work especially for the last two years," Eymard pleaded. "For more than four years that grace has been at work in my soul. I struggled against it, I feared it. I was afraid of the cross and of the suffering; all I ever wanted was permission to attend to this project for a while; I did not want to sever my bonds with the Marists which I love; besides, I did not want to foolishly lose a sure refuge.

"I see now that God is requiring of me to make a complete break, that I must even burn my bridges behind me. The sacrifice must be total. God is demanding full abandonment to His grace."

During what must have been for both men a most difficult and anguishing encounter, Father Eymard was able to
muster the strength needed to face his first major trial. He
searched deep into his soul only to find an equally uncompro-
mising God. But instead of being overwhelmed by what God
was asking of him, he recognized an invitation to follow a different path. God's grace would sustain him in spite of the in-
evitable sacrifices. It was clearer now than it ever was. The
road laid out before him led to the Eucharist. He had jour-
neyed along this road haltingly until now. For the first time
he realized he could not turn back. God had chosen him.

"It is done. I have decided."

With these simple words spoken to Fr. Favre, Eymard
cast his lot with the Lord. He would cut himself off from his
beloved Society of Mary where he was held in high esteem
and where he knew he could spend his life in the security of
this community and the adulation of his friends.

"You will quit the Marists?" exclaimed Fr. Favre.
"Yes," he replied, "I have been praying for a
long time. I implored our Lord, our Lady, and St.
Joseph to let me die rather than let me be deceived
or to go astray. All the time I felt myself urged on,
drawn only by the cross and the suffering it would
entail."
"In that case I can only let you go," said Fr.
Favre. "I will dispense you from your vows."

The two men separated, each one convinced that he had
acted according to the discernible will of God; the one in the
best interests of the Society of Mary while the other according to the unrelenting call of the Spirit.

Returning to his room, Father Eymard immediately wrote to his friend and colleague, Fr. De Cuers. "When Favre said to me: 'I will free you from your vows,' I was moved to tears and replied: 'Thank you.' For a moment we remained silent. The question was settled; nature was crucified but grace triumphed. At once I felt a sweet and mighty peace enter my soul; my heart was full of joy; God comforted me."

Some time later he wrote, "No one knows what it cost me to take that step and to say to God; 'Here I am; I left my natural family and my birthplace. I will leave my spiritual family to serve you in the Eucharist.'"

Before departing, Fr. Favre had requested that Eymard come to Lyons to receive the official written permission of dismissal from him personally. Anticipating strong and inevitably negative reactions from some of his Marist confreres, Father Eymard had written to De Cuers on April 25: "I dread a scene at Lyons at the moment of separation."

Well, his fears were not unfounded. When he arrived at Lyons he was literally bombarded with accusations of infidelity to his vocation and of giving sway to pride and ambition. So upset was he by this barrage from his confreres that he stayed awake all night. In the morning the first thing he did was to seek out Fr. Favre. The attacks by his fellow religious on his motives for leaving the Marists had shaken his resolve. Characteristically he decided that the only way out of this predicament was to present his case for the discernment of an independent judge. When he met Fr. Favre he shared with him what had happened and then told him that he wished to submit his situation to the judgment of an impartial person; and would he (Favre) mind not issuing the dispensation of his vows until this judgment were rendered. Favre willingly acceded to his request.

JUDGMENT IN PARIS

Traumatized by the negative outbursts of some of his Marist confreres which left him once again questioning his motives, he boarded the train for Paris in search of assurances. In the city he found lodging with a small religious community which was about to be dissolved. "They gave me a fireless room open to the wind," he wrote to a friend, "then another that was humid. At night the sheets were damp, as if they had been left out in the dew. The food was wretched. But God sustained me."

Thus began his retreat on May 1, 1856 the feast of the Ascension. With the recommendation of his friend, Bishop de la Bouillerie of Carcassonne, Father Eymard went to see Bishop Sibour, auxiliary of Paris and cousin of the archbishop with the same name, in order to explain his difficulty. The bishop told him to submit his case in writing so that he could study it and consult with the archbishop.

Eymard went back to his cold room and began writing.

"Allow me to open my soul to you about an idea that I believe comes from God. But, distrusting my own weakness and the illusions of self-conceit, I need your wise counsel that I may act in accordance with the ordinary ways of divine Providence, that is, by obedience."

He then proceeded to explain his situation and to promise to comply with the bishop's decision.

While awaiting a reply he wrote to a friend.

"I have opened my heart to a learned, experienced and tough man, with whom I was not previously acquainted. His final words to me were these; 'I must pray, reflect, and consult. Tuesday I will give you an answer.' What that answer will be, I don't know. I am somewhat reassured by the fact that I candidly related whatever was said against me at Lyons. I said too much to have any confidence left. But the will of God will be made known through him. If he tells me to give up the idea, I will do so knowing that I have acted according to my conscience. I am still on retreat alone, alone with our Lord. A little more prayer and patience and abandonment to God, and the whole thing will soon be over."

As convinced as he said he was of God's hand in this matter, he nevertheless remained skeptical about the outcome. He even told Fr. De Cuers, who had already arrived in Paris, that he had packed his bags and was ready to move back with the Marists as soon as he got the negative answer from the bishop. He had nothing left to do but to close his valises and to submit. De Cuers' reply was in the same vein: Like you, I only seek what our Lord wishes. I will go to Rome and end my days there.

Finally, on May 13, Father Eymard went to the archbishop's residence to receive the long awaited decision. De Cuers had arrived before him. So together they sat in the vestibule anxiously awaiting to be called by the bishop.

Here is how Eymard described what followed.

"We were waiting in the vestibule when the archbishop, who does not accompany his visitors that far, was obliged to come as far as the steps to show respect to Admiral Parceval who was just leaving. On the way back he noticed us and asked who we were and what was our business. We told him that we were awaiting Bishop Sibour. 'But what Bishop Sibour does here, cannot the archbishop do? What do you want?' So I told him about the decision we had come to receive. 'So you are a Marist priest?' 'Yes,' I replied. 'Bishop Sibour has told me all about it. No, no. It is purely contemplative. I am not in favor of those things. No, no.'

"I answered eagerly. 'That is not correct about our purpose. It is not a purely contemplative group. We adore, of course, but we wish to lead others also to adore. We would engage in the work of the First Communion of adults. We wish to inflame the four corners of France, and first the four corners of Paris, which needs it so much.' Upon hearing these words the archbishop's face lit up. 'The First Communion of adults,' he repeated, 'that is what I lack, the work I desire.' He seemed to be enthused."

The archbishop immediately took them by the arm and led them into his council room where Bishop Sibour and Fr. Carrière, the superior of St. Sulpice, were already waiting. He insisted that the matter must be discussed further. Father Eymard himself recounted what happened. "The archbishop described the work with words of praise. Bishop Sibour called it the crown of all the works of adoration in Paris. Fr. Carrière applauded it. The archbishop authorized it and approved it with fatherly kindness and said: 'Now you are my children.'"

Father Eymard, however, requested that they treat the question of the dispensation of his vows as a separate issue. They agreed to meet with him then on the following day. When he arrived the next day he was faced with three bishops. Bishop de la Bouillerie had been invited to take part in the discussion.

After Father Eymard had described in detail his spiritual

journey towards a Eucharistic vocation and the steps he had taken to test its authenticity, the three bishops agreed that divine Providence had indeed been at work in this matter and had guided the events which had brought him to their attention. They renewed their positive response of the previous day. Furthermore they gave Eymard the confirmation he had desperately sought in order to give himself wholeheartedly to the Eucharistic project and to set aside his uncertainties, hesitations, and indecision once and for all. Father Eymard heard the words he had come to Paris to hear.

The judgment of the three bishops could not have been more reassuring.

> "The will of God is clearly manifested in the Eucharistic work. God himself has settled the difficulty. You must consecrate yourself to this undertaking. There is no reason for further hesitation; you must go ahead."

That same evening he wrote to Fr. Favre.

> "After twelve days of waiting, of prayers, and of tears and abandonment, the trial is over at last. Twice I have received the answer that the will of God is that I devote myself to the work of the Blessed Sacrament.
>
> "I shall not recount the pains and temptations and trials which it pleased God to have me endure. Nor shall I tell you how much it cost my heart and soul and all of my feelings to take this step, this great step. For I see only the cross and the chalice, yet I am happy if God accepts my sacrifice. What I can tell you is that always, in heart and gratitude and filial devotion, I will be a child of the Society of

Mary.... How could I do otherwise than love a Society which has been so good and tender a mother to me."

Fr. Favre did not delay a reply, in a letter dated May 20 he wrote:

"Dear confrere. At last the affair is ended. May God's holy will, not ours, be done! All I can say is may God bless you and your work.... I beg you to continue to give me news of yourself, which will always be of great interest to me. Our separation from each other will not prevent our loving each other always in the hearts of Jesus and Mary."

Father Eymard now began a new journey, one that had been for so long a time unsure and unclear. Leaving the Marists was painful. Starting a new religious community would not give him any rest. In fact, exhausted from the stress and strain of negotiating his departure from the Marists and getting approval for the new Eucharistic project, he fell seriously ill with pneumonia and was obliged to seek rest with friends at their manor house in Leudeville, south of Paris.

This Eucharistic undertaking of Eymard's placed him in the midst of a virtual revival of devotion to the Blessed Sacrament occurring in the Church in France at the time. Even though people generally were still receiving Holy Communion infrequently, the seeds for a greater appreciation of the Eucharist had already been sown in many devotional practices. Father Eymard untiringly encouraged frequent Communion, contrary to current thinking and practice. A number of his contemporaries also promoted various Eucharistic devotions: Marie Tamisier would soon inaugurate the practice of Eucharistic Congresses; Hermann Cohen and Raymond de

Cuers had already launched the nocturnal adoration society; Mother Dubouche had established a Congregation of women dedicated to pray before the Blessed Sacrament.

Father Eymard's own special contribution to this increase of awareness of the value of the Eucharist in Christian life can perhaps be best expressed in his conviction that the Eucharist must be understood as the sure source of Catholic revival. It was this insight that now guided his life and which eventually became the keystone of his spiritual legacy.

Part Two

"Up till now, the Sun of the Eucharist
had not yet dawned.
But the full richness of the Eucharist
is unfolding before us.
It is truly amazing.
We perceive but a single Ray;
What will it be like later?"

Saint Peter Julian Eymard
September, 1861

Plaque commemorating the first SSS foundation on rue d'Enfer

Chapter Six

A New
Journey

"God will provide, it is His work."

FIRST COMMUNITY

At the end of May, 1856, Father Eymard returned to Paris from his short respite with his friends in Leudeville. He had spent some of his time revising the text of the Rule for the Blessed Sacrament Congregation. This was the same text he had sent to Rome earlier with Fr. Touche.

By June 1 he and Fr. De Cuers had moved into the sadly dilapidated building, on rue d'Enfer, which they had rented from the archdiocese with money from Fr. De Cuers' pension. Father Eymard at first refused to solicit money from the friends he had made during his long and successful ministry as a Marist for fear of offending his former confreres and in order to maintain good relations with the Society of Mary. "We have begun as one does in the wilderness," he wrote to a friend, "with two sheets, one chair, and one spoon, not two." Until they were able to purchase pots and pans they had to eat at a local restaurant. Two students, recent converts from

Judaism, who were about to enter the seminary gave them their furniture. At one point, a Sister from a nearby convent sent them a meal every day.

Although the archbishop paid for some basic repairs to the building both Fr. Eymard and Fr. De Cuers helped with the work in order to keep down the expenses. He wrote at the time: "We did manual labor, we waxed the floors, and carried materials for the workmen." By the end of September the little community numbered four people, two priests aided by a porter and a cook.

In spite of all their efforts their financial troubles only seemed to increase. One day the cook ran off with the money. Here is how Eymard described the situation in a letter to a friend.

> "We have had to bear another cross. A police commissioner, police officers, and a magistrate paid us a visit. We were being robbed daily by our cook. He had been using a duplicate key. The wretch is now in jail and will perhaps be sentenced to prison. I may have to appear at the trial. Imagine how painful this is for me. We smile at the incident, saying that the Good Lord perhaps thought that we were getting too wealthy. It is a hardship, but do not worry we will not starve. The thief took the money intended for the chapel. God will provide, it is His work."

By December the Cenacle, the name Father Eymard fondly used for the Eucharistic center, was practically finished. But the disciples did not come. A feeling of hopelessness overcame them. Yet, undaunted, Eymard wrote to a friend:

> "It is not for us to make vocations, but to receive them from the divine Goodness. The one who in-

vites is the King, not the servants. Ours is the happiness of having Jesus with us always. What could be a greater blessing? If the good Master wills that we remain alone for some months, for a year or even two years, blessed be His name. That's what will be best for us. What price is too great for this blessing of being His Eucharistic family? The world, even our friends, judging things only by success, numbers, achievement, will laugh at us or will consider us unproductive and discredited."

By Christmas two priests asked to be admitted to the fledgling Blessed Sacrament community. A date could now be set for the first public ceremony of exposition of the Blessed Sacrament. They settled on January 6, the feast of Epiphany. Bishop Hartmann of Bombay, visiting Paris at the time, presided at the memorable event.

In preparation for this special moment Father Eymard had made many personal sacrifices. It was at this time that he gave up wearing a small velvet skull cap which he wore as a protection against the recurrence of pleurisy and violent headaches. He also stopped wearing an arm band which was meant to protect him from certain chronic illnesses to which he was susceptible. As a final sacrifice he gave up the use of snuff.

"It was on December 8 that I asked the Blessed Virgin for the grace to give up tobacco and the use of a skull cap; and this good mother obtained the grace for me. Up to the present I am glad of it, and the privation is no longer a hardship. It is a little sacrifice, and near our Lord it will be more fitting."

A new calamity struck them, and all of Paris, when their supporter and friend, Archbishop Sibour, was stabbed to death by an assassin while presiding at devotions in the church of Saint Stephen. Father Eymard wrote at the time: "The archbishop's death has greatly affected us all. He was so good to us. This cruel death reminds us that God alone wishes to be our protector."

1857 — A YEAR OF DESOLATION

Throughout that first winter, poverty was their constant companion. They sold their personal books to keep from starving. Father Eymard's diary entries tell the story: "Thursday, February 26. No money. Friday, the 27th, Fr. De Cuers has fallen ill from grief. Saturday the 28th, Same. We have received no help from anyone." His prayer was desperate. "Lord Jesus, give me hope against hope."

Candidates came and went. Few stayed. Not once did the little community number more that six members at any one time. Everyone who came was without resources. And the expenses increased. To his friend, Marguerite Guillot, he wrote, "It is the hour of the suffering of Calvary. This is what makes me hope that the sacrifice will be blessed."

Spring did not bring them the promise of growth and sunshine. In the beginning of March the archdiocese informed them that they would have to find a new location because their property would be reclaimed by the new archbishop, Cardinal Morlot. They ran the risk of soon finding themselves among the 30,000 families left homeless because of the urban renewal projects underway to widen the boulevards of Paris and thus beautify the city. Weeks passed and nothing could be found. There were more buildings being destroyed to make Paris elegant than space available to house the displaced.

Father Eymard went almost daily in search of property. One night at the end of April, exhausted from walking the streets and discouraged at not finding anything, he returned to the little community only to discover that Fr. De Cuers had deserted him with no intention of returning. On that day he wrote in his diary,

> "We are now without any human support. I am in the greatest darkness, in a state of desolation."

Twenty-four hours later Fr. De Cuers returned, somewhat embarrassed by his precipitous behavior but ready to sail on in spite of the heavy winds against them. All summer long they continued to struggle in their poverty and uncertainty. Meanwhile Father Eymard's health deteriorated under the stress. In August he was forced to go away for treatment. He was away from his little community for five weeks and returned in September to a worsening state of affairs. The two postulants had left. Some local clergy had been slandering the little community, and even his old friend Fr. Hermann Cohen had turned against him and his new Society. The archbishop had heard vicious rumors about him and his little group. In October Father Eymard was summoned to the archbishop's residence to present his papers authorizing his Eucharistic project. After glancing at the documents which Eymard had handed him the archbishop gave them to his archpriest who claimed they had no official value and threw them into the waste basket.

Embarrassed and humiliated Father Eymard departed with an additional burden to carry, the rejection of the archbishop. He was so upset by the whole affair that he forgot to ask for his documents back. It took him a couple of days to muster enough courage to return and ask for his papers. They could not be found. He came back to the community totally distraught.

Some days later the archbishop's secretary appeared at

Eymard's doorstep to remedy the poor treatment he had received. He asked him to write down the events leading to his departure from the Marists and his subsequent launching of his Eucharistic work with the approval of the former archbishop. Father Eymard consented to do so. From that moment on the archbishop's attitude towards him changed dramatically even to the point where he would send his problem priests to Father Eymard with the injunction: "Do whatever he tells you, I do not know of a holier priest."

Father Eymard was overjoyed at the reconciliation which had taken place with the archbishop. His troubles, however, were still far from over. One day he learned that their residence had definitely been sold and that they would have to move by the beginning of the new year. After a painstaking search another property was finally found in the same neighborhood in the Faubourg Saint-Jacques. But negotiations broke down and by Christmas the little community of six still did not know if they would have a home by the new year.

On Christmas day he wrote to his friend and colleague Marguerite Guillot,

> "Last night I was in prayer from eleven o'clock to midnight; I was strong. Today, I could cry; it would make me feel better. Yesterday, on my way to the archbishop's house to discuss the matter of the property, I wept for the first time in a long time."

Finally, on February 19 the new property was purchased in Faubourg Saint-Jacques but it wasn't until Easter that they were able to move to their new quarters to celebrate the Eucharist and expose the Blessed Sacrament. At last the little community could settle down in its new Cenacle with some amount of serenity.

WORK OF FIRST COMMUNION AND EVANGELIZATION

The work of preparation for First Communion, especially among adults, was the aspect of the new Eucharistic venture that had interested the archbishop of Paris and for which he had granted his approbation to this new group. Other Eucharistic communities and organizations were springing up throughout France but Archbishop Sibour rightly perceived that Eymard's intuition about the Eucharist was not limited merely to the worship of the Holy Sacrament but to actively reach out to those who were estranged from the Church and to evangelize them. Father Eymard, however, directed his ministry first of all to the children and young workers who made up a large segment of the labor force of Paris.

He described this labor force from which he formed his catechism classes:

> "Those involved are children workers, vagabonds, or those placed in apprenticeship early and who have let the age of instruction for First Communion slip by... there are thousands of them in Paris. Rag-pickers, rope and match makers constituted the recruits from the workers' ranks; the rest were drawn from the ranks of the idlers, the indigent and beggars."

At the beginning Father Eymard collaborated with a devout layman Louis Perret, whom he had known in Lyons, in order to reach out to the young laborers of Paris. This layman, an architect by profession, took the initiative with some of his friends to enter the world of the workers by visiting factories and workshops and succeeded getting thirty young laborers to come for catechism classes. Later, as this apostolate grew, Eymard enlisted the collaboration of young people from the

Saint Vincent de Paul Society, also from others who came to him for spiritual direction, as well as a number of women friends who eventually worked with the women and the young girls.

For months Father Eymard struggled with a motley group of undisciplined young workers. They were disruptive, boisterous, and had a very short attention span. By dint of cajoling, giving small gifts, and even setting up a raffle he eventually won their confidence and respect. As soon as he was satisfied with their progress he allowed them to make their First Communion. Those that "graduated" had to recruit another student. He devised a raffle scheme based on a point system:

> "In order to maintain silence, attention and study from these young workers, we raffle… small articles of clothing, books, sweets. A large number of merit points gives them the right to something. These merit points… are given for attendance, for attention, and several for good recitations or explanations. The raffle following the Sunday of First Communion is the major one. It has more valuable items than the others and requires more merit points. This is the Recruiting Raffle…. The older the recruit [of those brought forward] the more merit points accorded…. This is our most effective means of recruiting, and the easiest."

In a letter to his friend Mr. Perret he once wrote that the raffle system is "still working wonders. Merit points are like California gold."

Another time he wrote about his work, "Our boys are missionaries of God. It is wonderful to see all they do to find other boys in the shops who have not made their First Communion. They then bring them over and encourage them to stay. They slip in everywhere with charming cleverness."

These young "missionaries" often recruited beyond their peers. Eymard recalls: "Many have brought their father or mother or sisters who had not made their First Communion. Through the children we have easy access to the parents who live without any religious practice and whose number is frighteningly great."

Father Eymard did not abandon his workers and ragpickers after their First Communion. He helped them form a workers club; and he would gather them for a yearly retreat. For the adults he planned setting up a reading library.

By the end of the first year over a hundred children and adults had made their First Communion. The program was so successful that ceremonies were held three times a year usually at Christmas, Easter and Assumption.

Because these young workers could attend catechism lessons only after work, their commitment had to be serious; and so the priests showed themselves most generous with their time and availability. To members of his Society Father Eymard one day said,

> "I am satisfied that our ministry does not possess any visible glamour. We are teaching fifty boys instead of taking our evening recreation. The good Lord sees it, that is enough.... If instead of these boys we had twelve princes to instruct, people would say, 'See what good these priests are doing. What a great Order it is.' For us these boys are twelve kings; they represent Jesus Christ, who said: 'As long as you did it to one of these, the least of my brothers, you did it to me.'"

One day upon seeing the large number of ragpickers

coming to his catechism classes Father Eymard said to his community,

> "The Congregation of the Blessed Sacrament has the most beautiful aim to which a religious Order can aspire. Hence it must have the most beautiful mission: to raise up what is most wretched and depraved. We could not find anything lower than the ragpickers of Paris. Now we have many of them. It is a beautiful mission. It recalls our Lord's second invitation to come to the Eucharist. The first was to the great ones who refused. They were more concerned with their own affairs than with the feast of the king's son. What did the king say? He said: 'Go out quickly into the streets and the alleys of the city and bring in the poor, the feeble, the lame, and the blind.' And the servant said: 'Lord it is done as you have ordered but there is still room.' And the Lord said to the servant: 'Go out into the highways and hedges and compel them to come in.' Such has been our first ministry. Indeed, what took place at the beginning is probably our mission."

In another of his diary entries he described how he had been moved to tears so happy was he at seeing thirty-seven adults make their First Communion on the feast of the Assumption. At Christmas he preached and celebrated Mass for forty-two young adults who, in attendance with their families, were taking Holy Communion for the first time. After the ceremony "there was lunch, composed of sausages, pie, stewed apples, bread and wine." At three o'clock they received Confirmation, and Benediction of the Blessed Sacrament followed. "Then they received their souvenirs and rosary. The weather was bad, with snow all day."

Father Eymard did not limit his concern to purely spiritual matters. He also found decent clothing for his First Communicants so they would not be embarrassed when they came to church; he offered them food and beverage after classes; he even provided them with small gifts to remind them of how special they were and that they should not forget the day of their First Communion.

This picture of Father Eymard caring for the spiritual and material needs of his "tramps," as some wealthy ladies who attended the chapel were fond of calling them, is sharply contrasted with statements by certain churchmen of the day. In a pastoral letter the bishop of Paris wrote: "To you, the poor, we bring the hopes of religion as a wonderful compensation for what fortune denies you and a powerful motive for resignation and patience." In another pastoral letter, this time by the bishop of Bayonne, the message is the same: "To the poor, the needy, to all those who worry about lacking the necessities of life, Religion says: 'Why so much worry, why such concern?... Does not your heavenly Father know what is good for you?' It is enough for you to bear the misfortune which oppresses you with resignation, with courage, with gratitude, even with joy...."

As the program grew and developed so did the expenses. When he inaugurated a three day retreat for the adults prior to making their Holy Communion, he found himself obliged to pay some of the salaries of the workers who could not afford to take time away from work for a retreat. He also committed himself to paying for their food during the retreat days. Consequently, a couple of times a year Father Eymard went preaching for financial help in some of the more prominent churches of Paris. He was not too proud to beg in order to support his ministry. He also "slipped in a few delicate words" in his correspondence to solicit funds from his friends.

He was not embarrassed to befriend the wealthy in order to provide them an opportunity to assist the poor and to participate in his ministry. An entire list of prominent women came to his aid, such as the Countess d'Andigne, Madame de Fraguier, Madame Wiriot, and Madame de la Bouraliere. Some of these women were widows who had either funds or time which they generously shared for the benefit of a religious cause.

A story is told which illustrates Father Eymard's apostolic sensitivity and how he easily adapted to the pressing needs of people. One day a young couple came to see him. They were ragpickers and they could only meet with him in the evening. So he met them at night when the religious of the community were already asleep. He instructed them so that they could make their Holy Communion, which they did, and later he blessed their marriage. On that day he provided them with a meal and served it himself.

Although he ministered preferentially to the ragpickers and laborers, he did not ignore anyone who would ask for religious instructions. He also baptized and prepared for the sacraments a number of converts from other faiths, Protestants and Jews.

Stories abound about these early days of the Congregation. A touching account of a conversion is told of a young eighteen-year-old stonemason who claimed to have lived like an animal until he was instructed in the faith and received his Holy Communion. Being illiterate he would pay a fellow laborer one penny a day to teach him how to read so that he could study his catechism. The day of his First Communion he went home to his blind mother and kissed and hugged her promising how much better he would behave now that he had made his Communion, so happy was he. His mother became very sad.

"What is the matter?" he asked her. She burst into tears.

"Are you not happy that I have made my Holy Communion?"

"Yes, I am indeed," she replied, "but I can't help crying because I myself have never made my First Communion. I am so unworthy."

Amidst his own tears the son promised to teach his mother the lessons of the catechism he himself had just mastered. Every night after work the son would promptly go to his mother to have her repeat the catechism lessons. "One day the two of them came to see me," recounted Father Eymard, "and she told me she was ready to confess for the first time. She explained how she had cried the day her son had made his Holy Communion because he was so happy and that she too wanted to make her Holy Communion. When the day came, the two of them knelt side by side to receive the God of all consolation. I cannot describe the joy that filled both of them that day."

Father Eymard also spent time visiting the neighborhood in which he lived. He was often seen in a number of districts which were considered unsafe and somewhat dangerous. On one occasion Father Eymard, accompanied by a Brother, ventured into one of these districts, this particular one was called Lion's Den, to which he had been summoned to administer the sacraments. As soon as they arrived in the area a group of people began to shout insults at the two of them. Suddenly a few boys whom he had prepared for Holy Communion recognized him and came running to rescue him. The crowd settled down and he proceeded to the house to which he had been called and administered the sacrament of baptism. The boys in the district used to say: "In our neighborhood we don't even see policemen; they don't dare come around here. But we often see Father Eymard."

Many years later he wrote from Belgium to a friend that he would like to see this apostolate extend to many areas of Paris, "and finally here" in Brussels. In fact, Father Eymard had written in his Constitutions that this work of the First Communion of adults should be the apostolate of his Society.

LADIES FROM LYONS

Soon after Father Eymard had settled with Fr. De Cuers in Paris he contacted some of the women from Lyons whom he had known and with whom he had worked when he was director of the Third Order of Mary. The director of the women's branch of the Third Order was Marguerite Guillot, a very devout and competent young woman who with her three sisters operated a specialized mending and ironing business and in which establishment Marguerite managed the financial accounts. Marguerite had selected Father Eymard as her spiritual adviser and he in turn had been struck by her profound religious spirit and her ardent devotion.

Consequently, he turned to her when he realized that the First Communion project would soon involve the catechetical preparation of young girls for this sacrament. He had been assisted already by some women who had come to Paris from Toulon and who had been for some time participating in a Eucharistic adoration prayer group directed by the Marists there. Father Eymard, however, wanted to establish something more directly linked to his new Congregation, namely, a women's branch of the Blessed Sacrament Congregation. This is what he had in mind when he asked Marguerite to come to Paris. She arrived with her sister, Claudine, and a friend, Benoîte, in May of 1858.

Initially, Father Eymard had both groups of women combined to form a single community and placed Marguerite in charge despite her persistent objections. He had confided with Marguerite his vision of "one church for priests and sisters" where there would be "only one Exposition" for both groups. This would recall "the church where the Apostles, the disciples, the holy women and Mary prayed together in the first church at the foot of the first tabernacle." For the next six years the women shared their prayer life in a common chapel with the priests and the people.

In the morning after their personal prayer time these women prepared young girls for First Communion. They remained in lay clothes and were popularly known by the local poor people as the Ladies (Dames) of the Blessed Sacrament.

Some years later Father Eymard formed them into a religious community and moved them to Angers. There they donned a religious habit and took on the name of Sister Servants of the Blessed Sacrament; a name which he told them described Mary's own life in the Cenacle with the apostles. However much he wanted them to accept the name of Servants, to the poor people in Paris they were always known as the Ladies (catechists) of the Blessed Sacrament.

The community prospered in spite of its many material hardships and the heavy burdens encountered by the new religious Congregation. Father Eymard continued to inspire them by his frequent retreat talks and conferences. With regards to the Congregation's development, however, Marguerite proved to be a courageous leader who suffered greatly to give life to her community. To her spiritual daughters she was affectionately called Mother Marguerite.

"A PURELY CONTEMPLATIVE LIFE CANNOT BE FULLY EUCHARISTIC"

There was a priest in Lyons, Fr. Antoine Chevrier, who had committed himself to a similar apostolate of preparing poor children for First Communion. One day Father Eymard enthusiastically communicated to Fr. De Cuers that he had received a letter from Chevrier and he (Eymard) used the occasion to emphasize how important he considered this apostolate.

> "I have just received a letter from this saintly priest whom I know. I'm pleased. I like the work of First Communion. It's the fruit of the Eucharistic banquet. There has to be some activity associated with adoration."

Some time later Father Eymard wrote again to De Cuers to explain his desire to expand this work of First Communion and how he thought it might be accomplished by combining his efforts with those of Chevrier who expressed his wish to join the Blessed Sacrament Community.

> "Five days ago I went to Lyons. Fr. Chevrier wanted to see me so that I could see the situation and the people firsthand. I spent 24 hours there and saw no one else. I was quite edified by Fr. Chevrier who accepts the Congregation without reservations and wants to give himself to it completely.... Fr. Chevrier has this wonderful ministry of First Communion to which he has already committed a few years. His building is set up to receive poor children. They are like his own children. He keeps them for

two or three months depending on their disposition and behavior. He is doing really good work and it is being well received. We too need a ministry that can engage our Eucharistic zeal, otherwise our adorers will waste their time when not occupied.... A purely contemplative life cannot be fully Eucharistic. A raging fire has a flame."

However hard both men tried to join forces it never came about, not because of differences of vision among themselves but simply because the archbishop of Lyons refused to give up one of his most respected and holy priests to a newly founded religious community which he had not yet welcomed into his own archdiocese. Father Eymard also had hoped that this union could have brought his new Congregation to Lyons. Father Chevrier himself subsequently founded a Religious Congregation of priests to work for the poor by living among them. He was beatified in 1986.

FIRST TRIP TO ROME

By the end of 1858, after two years of struggling to survive, the small community in the Faubourg Saint-Jacques numbered twelve members, seven priests and five brothers. Together they had labored at establishing this little Cenacle as an oasis in the thriving and noisy capital of France. Throughout Father Eymard and his disciples continued their First Communion ministry to the underprivileged while maintaining an active prayer life contemplating the Holy Eucharist in their small chapel to which they invited priests and people to share some brief moments of their lives in the refreshing presence of the Blessed Sacrament. Fr. De Cuers was especially involved in promoting nocturnal adoration, a practice of praying at night, which he had launched earlier with Fr. Cohen, a renowned pianist and Jewish convert.

Heartened by these small apostolic steps taken by his community Father Eymard boldly decided it was time to request some kind of formal recognition from Rome for his Blessed Sacrament community. So long as he had only the approval of the archbishop of Paris his little group could not easily expand to other dioceses. De Cuers was already looking to Marseilles as the site for a possible second community. Brussels too was clamoring for a foundation. By November of 1858 Eymard had already drafted a petition to be presented to the Holy Father requesting official Vatican approbation. But first he needed to have this petition endorsed by several bishops.

As soon as he could manage he visited a number of bishops to seek their support. His request was met with enthusiasm. He was able to enlist the support of the bishop of Grenoble, his home diocese; the archbishop of Lyons, where he worked for many years and was respected; Bishop Wicart of Laval, an old friend; Bishop de Mazenod who was hoping to get the Blessed Sacrament community to settle in his own diocese; and, of course, the archbishop of Paris who declared that the priests and brothers at the Cenacle were well deserving of the Church's blessing because of their deep devotion to the Eucharist and their proven apostolic zeal.

Armed with these glowing testimonials Father Eymard set out for Rome and arrived there on December 8 (1858) to lodge at the French seminary. He wrote to Marguerite Guillot, "Here I am in Rome. I arrived without mishap and without much pain. I was not even seasick. I celebrated Mass at the tomb of St. Catherine of Siena in the Dominican church of St. Mary, Minerva." After celebrating the Eucharist he went directly to St. Peter's and entered the basilica on his knees. He shared his impressions in a letter,

"When you enter St. Peter's you are overwhelmed with faith and devotion which lifts you towards Jesus Christ. Words simply have no power to express what you experience in your heart. You are so proud to be a Catholic. I was thrilled to pray at the tomb of St. Peter and to have celebrated Mass in the crypt which has been venerated by Christians for centuries."

On December 20 Father Eymard was escorted into the presence of Pope Pius IX. After their meeting, he wrote to a friend, "I have seen the Holy Father. He blessed us and granted us precious indulgences. He was most kind to me and promised to review my petition to which he will give us a reply in two weeks time. So now we must pray."

During the ensuing two weeks Father Eymard doubled his prayers. He would return often to pray at St. Peter's basilica. He himself recounts an incident which transpired one day during one of these visits:

"One day, it was January 5, I came to the Confession of St. Peter. It was evening and there were a lot of visitors. I knelt at one of the pillars and became so absorbed in my prayers that all the noise and distractions around me vanished. I have no idea how long I remained in this condition but I know that it lasted a fairly long time.… When I regained awareness of my surroundings everything was quiet and there were no more visitors. I turned around to leave and there kneeling at his prie-dieu, just a short distance behind me, was the Holy Father. He was about to depart. He had entered with his entire retinue of Swiss guards, and I had heard nothing. I was quickly escorted away by one of the Swiss guards ostensibly annoyed at this gawking priest standing there in front of the Pope."

The following day he received the "Writ of Praise," a document marking the first step leading to full approbation of a Religious Congregation which can only be requested after a Congregation has established at least three religious communities. It had been signed by the Pope himself.

Father Eymard acted quickly upon the new status which the "Writ of Praise" had granted his little community. He promptly returned to Paris and after making a week's retreat each member of the new Blessed Sacrament Community professed their vows. On that day, Wednesday, March 2, 1859 they all gathered in the chapel and after singing the *Veni Creator* to invoke the blessings of the Holy Spirit, Father Eymard addressed them and placed the monstrance containing the Blessed Sacrament upon the altar. Then, kneeling before the Holy Sacrament, he was the first to pronounce his vows to God as a religious of the Blessed Sacrament. Each one then in turn did the same.

Thus the Cenacle in Faubourg Saint-Jacques became the mother house of the Congregation of the Blessed Sacrament. The very next day Fr. De Cuers left for Marseilles to look for some property in order to set up a second community.

Fr. Antoine Chevrier

Fr. De Cuers and Fr. Eymard

CHAPTER SEVEN

A Journey Inward

"...approved, but not yet sanctified."

DE CUERS - MARSEILLES

Negotiations had taken place with the bishop of Marseilles, Bishop de Mazenod, long before Fr. De Cuers arrived in that city to set up a community. Marseilles was a city which he had known very well as a naval officer and as the diocese in which he had established the nocturnal adoration society some years previously. For many years the Marseilles foundation was characterized by the particular stamp given to it by Fr. De Cuers. Its community life was tightly organized and its program of adoration of the Blessed Sacrament was highly structured. This foundation more than any of the others, even during the time of the founder, maintained the richness of the Exposition services and emphasized the royal dimension of the divine presence in its chapel. It was here that for the first time that the royal mantle, long associated with the Congregation of the Blessed Sacrament, was used to enhance the kingly aspect of Eucharistic exposition. Here in Marseilles was inaugurated the Aggregation of the Blessed Sacrament, an organization of lay people who were associated with the aims of the Congregation and whose members promised to spend one hour of prayer a month before the Blessed Sacrament. The first public devotion expressed to Mary under the title of Our Lady of the Blessed Sacrament began here.

The little money which he had, Fr. De Cuers spent on decorating the chapel. He persuaded Eymard to send him a carpenter from Paris to do some woodwork in the sanctuary. He soon ran out of funds, but he had traveled with poverty before. In Paris during the rough years of the first foundation it had not been poverty that had driven him away; he never gave much thought to his own personal well being. In fact his one and only cassock was in such a bad condition that he was unable to leave the house. At times friends insisted that he take a meal with them because they knew he was not eating properly.

The archbishop was made aware of Fr. De Cuers' situation and he personally wrote to Eymard inviting him to come and preach in his cathedral to raise some funds for his poor community in Marseilles. Father Eymard readily accepted. The Vicar General of the diocese sent a letter to all of the pastors announcing the event and reminded them that this letter should be read in their churches. At the end of the letter the Vicar General remarked that at the end of the ceremony a collection would be taken. The bishop would preside.

Fr. De Cuers' zeal for embellishing the throne of exposition was unmatched even by the founder. On opening day a large heraldic royal mantle of red velvet with ermine facing and dominated by a gilded crown was set as a backdrop for the monstrance above the altar. The simplicity of the Paris chapel stood in sharp contrast to the princely decor of Marseilles.

There is no evidence that the community in Marseilles

ever inaugurated the apostolate of First Communion among the poor street children or for adults. On the contrary, the Marseilles community took on the distinctive stamp of its superior, Fr. De Cuers, for whom the Blessed Sacrament was the Lord and the King who required attention day and night. De Cuers, always the naval officer, organized a structure to maintain an uninterrupted service of prayer before the Blessed Sacrament somewhat along the lines of the rotating "watch" on a ship. The community of Paris, on the other hand, under the inspiration of Father Eymard, developed differently along more apostolic lines. Years later, when Fr. De Cuers succeeded Eymard as Superior General and when the Paris community moved to the other side of the Seine river, it soon left the poor behind. From that time onward the Marseilles community became the model for the Blessed Sacrament Congregation, and the Founder's fervor for the poor and the work of First Communion vanished.

The new Congregation attracted the attention of many bishops and a number of them invited Father Eymard to establish a community in their diocese. One of the first to inquire was the bishop of Arras who wanted a Eucharistic community devoted to reparation. Eymard refused this invitation because he did not want to limit the scope of his Congregation merely to the aspect of reparation.

Then there followed a foundation at Angers where the nocturnal adoration society had existed since 1850, and daytime adoration since 1854. In that same year the practice of perpetual adoration of the Blessed Sacrament in different parishes each day of the year had been inaugurated. The bishop himself had founded a group of priests, whom the people christened "priests of adoration", who would go about preaching retreats and missions in the churches of the diocese. In December 1862 the Angers community was established. Fr. Eymard arrived with five religious from Paris and stayed for about a week. He was very fond of the Angers foundation. He wrote in a letter to the Countess d'Andigne how he loved to pray in the Angers chapel where at the feet of the Master he would "forget Paris, Marseilles, La Mure."

Father Eymard would return to Angers often to preach and to conduct retreats. He was a very popular preacher there where the faith of the people was strong as was their devotion to the Blessed Sacrament. Eymard's retreats were so well attended that he feared the neighboring pastors would become upset at seeing their parishioners absent from their parishes on Sunday mornings for the closing of the retreat. Having been a pastor himself Father Eymard did not feel slighted by the legitimate concerns of dedicated parish priests. One Sunday at the closing of a retreat he climbed the pulpit and addressed the people:

> "My dear brethren, I am very happy to see all of you here but I strongly urge you to attend Mass in your own parish churches at least on Sunday. Duty prevails over piety. We have not come here to replace the parish priests, but simply to collaborate with them…. I also have been a parish priest and loved my parish a lot."

BACK TO ROME

Now that there were three communities functioning, Father Eymard lost no time in applying to Rome for final and definitive approval for his Congregation. Pope Pius IX was ailing and Father Eymard did not want to risk a new start with his successor. Pius IX had shown himself so well disposed towards the Blessed Sacrament Congregation that Father

Eymard pushed ahead to obtain the pontiff's approval in spite of few vocations.

Many candidates had come to test their calling but most of them did not persevere. One day a young man by the name of Auguste Rodin arrived and asked to be admitted to the community. Father Eymard accepted him and soon noticed his artistic inclination and allowed him the use of a small studio adjoining the garden. Now and then he would go there and sit with the young artist to discern whether he had a calling to religious life. It was most probably during these visits that Rodin sculptured a remarkable bust of Father Eymard. Eventually Auguste Rodin found his true vocation in the art world; so did his artistic creation, a masterpiece in bronze of his spiritual mentor.

Eymard left for Rome on March 9, 1863 accompanied by Fr. De Cuers and a postulant who had been a long time friend from Paris. It was this friend who had provided the Paris Cenacle with its first monstrance and who had now offered to pay for this journey to the eternal city. This friend was the same Mr. de Leudeville who had welcomed Eymard during his illness some years back.

For three days they tossed about on angry seas between Marseilles and Civitavecchia. Father Eymard, not having the stomach of his naval companion, was sick the whole voyage. In Rome they stayed with the Holy Cross Fathers who administered the chapel of St. Bridget in the Piazza Farnese, where there was exposition of the Blessed Sacrament. The three of them followed the Holy Week services in the holy city. The petition had been presented to the Holy Father but no word was forthcoming. Eymard prayed. Fr. De Cuers and Mr. de Leudeville visited the churches of Rome. April and May came and went without an answer.

Meanwhile, on the political front trouble was brewing in the land. King Victor Emmanuel was mustering an army in the Piedmont in the north. In the south Garibaldi was plotting the takeover of the Papal States while French troops remained stationed in Rome to protect their interests and to defend the pope and his territorial claims. In the end the French effort was futile because the Papal States eventually were absorbed into a unified Italy. Consequently, the Holy Father, already in ill health and preoccupied with maintaining his hold on the papal territories, could not attend to Eymard's humble petition.

Eventually Father Eymard inquired discreetly about the delay and whether there was anything he could do to expedite the matter. He was advised to speak with the cardinal in charge of these matters, which he did. The cardinal informed him that the reasons for the delay were that someone had come forward with accusations against him. Father Eymard was speechless. "What kind of accusation?" The question was asked haltingly, not out of fear of hearing the reply, but out of sheer disbelief that the words had been spoken at all.

The cardinal responded that Eymard had been accused first of leaving the Marists without authorization; and second that the residence of his Blessed Sacrament Community in Paris was actually connected to the building which housed women catechists.

Father Eymard vehemently denied these calumnies and protested strongly. He produced documentation proving that everything had been done properly and in good order. After examining the documents the cardinal assured him that he would discuss the matter with the Holy Father. Eymard was then promised a quick resolution to this unfortunate affair. In the meantime Eymard's accuser was himself denounced and made to apologize. Since nothing happens quickly in Rome, Father Eymard had time to make a retreat at the Passionist Monastery while awaiting a reply to his petition.

Finally, on June 10, he received the long awaited Decree of Approbation. In part it read:

> "The above named priest, Eymard... has presented to the Holy Father, Pope Pius IX, his humble petition for the approval of the religious Congregation....
>
> "His Holiness approves and confirms by this Decree this Congregation... of the Blessed Sacrament as an institute with simple vows under the authority of a Superior General... leaving to a future time the approval of the Constitutions regarding which the Holy Father seeks to make a few corrections.
>
> Given in Rome... June 3, 1863."

It had been a long journey; all the pain, the wrenching departure from his Marist community, the poverty, the lack of vocations, and the last minute accusations which nearly derailed the whole project... it was all behind him now.

With the Decree of Approbation in hand and gratitude in his heart he hurried to share his joy with Fr. De Cuers who, upon scanning the document, broke into a rage waving the document in Eymard's face shouting,

"What is your name doing on this Decree?"

All along De Cuers had rejected every personal recognition in regard to the foundation of the Blessed Sacrament Congregation. He was seemingly not objecting to the absence of his own name on the document; rather, he would not tolerate any personal acknowledgment of any sort. All recognition belonged exclusively to the Lord and Master.

Whatever were De Cuers' motives for the outburst, it caused Father Eymard great suffering and strained their relationship. The two men were temperamentally very different. De Cuers, with his naval training, seemed more secure with a highly disciplined and ordered style of life. He was intensely motivated but often narrow and simplistic in his approach. The story is told of how he would exit the church backwards when the Blessed Sacrament was exposed so as not to turn his back to the Master. Another time, in Paris, Father Eymard had allowed the young religious to sit down in the sanctuary during their prayers. When Fr. De Cuers saw the chairs which had been provided for this purpose, he personally threw them out of the sanctuary claiming more discipline and austerity were required.

Their relationship was built perhaps more on a common, though equally profound, attraction to the Eucharist than on friendship or even on complete agreement concerning the means to be taken to make the Blessed Sacrament better known and loved. In any case, this incident did not help ameliorate their relationship; in point of fact, it very likely aggravated an already frayed one.

Perhaps the best conclusion to this episode is a line which Fr. Eymard wrote a few months later,

"Well, we have been approved, but we have not yet been sanctified."

CONSTITUTIONS

The rift between Father Eymard and Fr. De Cuers continued to widen. On their return to France they held a meeting in Paris of all the religious to consider matters of interest to the whole group. One issue under discussion was whether the Congregation would admit lay candidates as Brothers. Fr. De Cuers argued forcefully that the Congregation should be limited to priest members only. Father Eymard insisted that both groups should be welcomed. After some time for discussion a secret vote was taken and the issue was decided overwhelmingly in favor of accepting Brothers. De Cuers returned to Marseilles and Eymard set about re-editing the text of the Constitutions of the Congregation which Rome had requested.

Before putting the final touches on the text of the Constitutions Father Eymard consulted the Rules of other religious groups, such as the Jesuits, the Dominicans, the Carmelites, and the Benedictines of Solesme. He was tireless in pursuit of this task. He traveled extensively to get the best advice possible.

Despite his illness, for which he had to take water treatments, he continued working as is evident from his correspondence. From the hotel Bossuet where he was staying he wrote that he was profiting from this respite to organize the research he had collected so far. He didn't get better. So finally he took Fr. Chanuet's advice and accepted an invitation to spend some quiet time at the chateau of Chanuet's brother-in-law at St. Bonnet-le-Froid in the hills outside of Lyons.

On October 6, 1863, he wrote to Mrs. Chanuet, Fr. Chanuet's mother, explaining how much he appreciated being at the chateau. He compared it to "the holy cave of St. Benedict, Francis' Mount Alverno, the Manresa of Ignatius... even better, my peaceful Cenacle. Besides I can work peacefully here." On the same day he wrote to Fr. De Cuers:

> "Here I am with the family of Father Chanuet amidst a great and charming solitude, the Blessed Sacrament, and a saintly family. The good Lord has provided this for me so that I can rest and do some work. I've already started and I hope God will give

me the grace to continue. I'm starting to sleep again. My coughing is lessening and my pulse is getting more regular. Don't worry about me, offer a prayer for me and ask others to do the same so that on this mountain I may be united to Our Lord and be able to write under His inspiration."

A few days later, on the 11 of October, he sent another letter to Fr. De Cuers commenting on his health and the wonderful environment he had found.

"I'm doing much better. This respite at St. Bonnet complements the water treatments that I now see as having been beneficial. I am here amidst peace, solitude and piety. I'm working like I've never worked before... I needed this time and this tranquillity. I hope you will thank God with me for this. I think I'll stay here until I finish the Constitutions and the Directory. I have half my work completed and the services of a good secretary."

As a result of his time at St. Bonnet, the text of the Constitutions returned from the printer within a matter of months. Father Eymard presented a copy to each member of the Congregation with these words:

"Your conduct and behavior must approve this Rule before it is approved from on high. The Church wants to see if you can live by it; if not, why bother getting it approved! This Rule is not characterized by any divine or heavenly inspiration other than having as its aim the service of Our Lord in the Blessed Sacrament by a group of men dedicated solely to Him."

JERUSALEM

Father Eymard now sought to establish the fourth foundation of the Congregation. Encouraged by the strong support of Fr. De Cuers he turned towards Jerusalem. What more appropriate place for the next community than the Cenacle where Jesus had broken bread with his disciples and enjoined them to "do this in memory of Me."

On January 6, 1864, Fr. De Cuers along with a young theology student by the name of Albert Tesniere set sail for Jerusalem. They made a stop in Rome to obtain papers of introduction and then set off again on their journey. Neither of them anticipated the fact that it would be impossible even to propose a possible purchase of the Cenacle from the Moslems, in whose hands it was, and for whom the place was equally sacred because it housed the tomb of King David. As soon as they realized that there would be no question of obtaining the Cenacle they settled on purchasing a site near to it. But first they had to return to Rome to obtain permission.

Once in Rome, Fr. De Cuers in his customary straightforward manner made it clear to everyone that he was hoping to be granted permission to buy property in Jerusalem for the purpose of establishing a religious community near the Cenacle. The word spread quickly throughout Rome even without benefit of postal or telephone services just as it had done for centuries.

The Franciscans, who had exclusive rights to ministry in the Holy Places, protested vehemently to protect their privileged position in Jerusalem. As a direct consequence of their intervention the Eucharistic project for Jerusalem came to a standstill.

In November, Father Eymard set out for Rome to attempt himself to negotiate the Jerusalem foundation. Little progress was made. Days turned into weeks and then months. Finally on March 29, 1865, he received a definitive answer. There would be no foundation in Jerusalem. He accepted the decision as being the Will of God. He returned to Paris the following day.

RETREAT AT ROME

It was during this extended stay in Rome awaiting an answer to the Jerusalem question that Father Eymard used the occasion to make a long retreat, from January to the end of March, at the Redemptorist monastery. This long retreat proved as decisive for his spiritual life as the decision about Jerusalem proved definitive for that foundation. The opening lines of his retreat notes reveal his disposition. The aim of this retreat would be "to work at my personal sanctification."

Towards the end of the retreat Father Eymard made what he described the "vow of his personality" to God. This gift of his very being was the ultimate act of abandonment. All of his life he had offered God bits and pieces of himself: his good works, his heart, his will, even his failures. With the "gift of self" he was now declaring his willingness that God be completely and totally in charge of his entire life and of his whole person. This gift required that he allow the Holy Spirit to transform him. From this moment he placed himself into God's molding hands. He realized that progress in holiness depended much less on the efforts one made, as heroic as these may be at times, but rather on the intensity and the completeness with which God takes hold of the person and directs his or her life.

For years he had lived as if progress in the spiritual life depended, if not solely at least to a major extent, on the strength of his will. Personal discipline, he had thought, was proof of a strong will and consequently of God's strength.

Now he knew that he merely had to let God take over. To place his salvation on the strength of his own will left salvation in his hands, not in God's. With the "gift of self" he would allow God to take charge of him.

This retreat proved to be pivotal in his life as it provided him with a profound insight into the dynamics of his own soul. He had succeeded to free himself from an excessive preoccupation with individual acts of the will as a gauge of spiritual progress.

When he left Rome he did not go by sea this time but directly north via Turin because he could no longer tolerate being sick at sea.

The chapel and steeple at St. Bonnet de Froid

Part Three

"The mason who dies after laying the
foundation of a colossal structure
is more of a founder than
the one who completes it."

Saint Peter Julian Eymard
November, 1866

Shrine of Our Lady of La Salette today

Chapter Eight

A Consuming Journey

"...let the rain fall."

FIRST GENERAL ASSEMBLY

Father Eymard's decision to return to his country overland in order to avoid the sleepless nights and the debilitating days with which he had to battle whenever he had to sail, did not leave him entirely without discomfort. The coach rides were exceedingly bumpy and dusty. He arrived in Lyons, after a brief visit with his sister in La Mure, completely exhausted and took refuge in the home of one of his dear friends, Mrs. Jordan and her family. By the middle of April 1865 he was back in Paris after being away from his community, with the Jerusalem business, for over five months. On the 22nd of that month he wrote,

> "I have plunged again into the world of visits and business. May God be praised. I'm a bit annoyed, however, because as soon as I arrived I caught the flu which forced me to stay at home and drag myself about."

The first urgent business was to convoke a general meeting of all the vowed members of the Congregation in order to finalize the text of the Constitutions and to proceed with the election of a Superior General. He wrote to each member to alert them of the meeting to be held in the Paris community and to advise them of the agenda.

His correspondence during this period provides an insight into the disposition of his soul as this historic meeting neared. To Mrs. Andigne he wrote,

"The general assembly... for the election of the Superior will take place on July 3. I hope thereby to be freed from this heavy burden and happily find myself as a simple religious with only myself to worry about; I have been struggling for eight years. Just a place at the feet of Our Lord... would refresh this poor soul caught up with so many preoccupations."

In a letter to Fr. Chanuet he shared similar sentiments,

"During the four years leading up to the foundation [of the Congregation] I experienced every possible trial. Now the Congregation is approved and on its way; my mission is accomplished."

To his long time collaborator, Fr. De Cuers, with whom he had traveled from the first days of the founding of the Congregation and whose friendship had been at times as turbulent as the sea voyages he had preferred to avoid, he wrote,

"Allow me the consolation of remaining but a simple religious with some solitude. Someone else can now lead the Congregation.... One sows, another reaps! I ask you as a great favor and out of friendship not to consider me for the position. I will obey whomsoever is elected as representing Jesus Christ."

After three days of retreat in preparation for the general meeting Father Eymard was elected Superior for life, over his own entreaties and Fr. De Cuers' resentment, receiving all the votes but one. He was so sure of not being selected that when the results were announced he asked to be excused, so overwhelmed was he by the outpouring of trust and confidence in his leadership. He retired in solitude to his quarters while the others went to the chapel to sing a *Te Deum* in gratitude to God.

Resigned to what he clearly perceived as the will of God and the overwhelming wish of his confreres, he courageously shouldered the care and development of the Congregation which he described to Marguerite Guillot as "crushing."

In addition to the business of the Congregation he was also worried about his sister, Marianne, who had fallen seriously ill. He wrote to her on the 16th of July, 1865:

"The news that you were sick saddened me. I couldn't run off to La Mure because I was in a General Chapter... for ten days straight I didn't have a free moment. I prayed hard to Our Lord, dear sister, to comfort you and to cure you; I only have you left on this earth. I realize that heaven is preferable to this poor existence.... I don't know when I'll be free but I do plan to visit you soon, probably in a fortnight."

On August 1st he visited his ailing sister whose condition improved slightly after he made a three day pilgrimage to the shrine of Our Lady of La Salette to pray for her. After about a week he returned to Paris only to discover that her condition had worsened and as soon as he was able to clear his work he rushed to La Mure to be with her. In a letter to Marguerite Guillot, dated September 8, 1865, he wrote,

> "This morning I celebrated Mass in her room and gave her Communion; she was delighted, and so was I. This afternoon she suffered greatly and this evening she is completely exhausted. My poor sister.... Heaven seems to be calling for her."

Three days later, on Monday the eleventh, he went to the shrine of Our Lady of La Salette again to entreat Mary for help on behalf of his sister. From there he traveled south to the shrine of Our Lady of Laus and wrote a few days later,

> "We were at Our Lady of Laus on Wednesday 13 when my sister nearly died; but she recovered after a three hour serious relapse.
> "She is now doing better, her cough stopped when we returned from Our Lady of Laus. That night I applied some of the oil from the sanctuary lamp from Laus. She had a peaceful night and the next morning she wasn't coughing. From that time I would apply the blessed oil, and with the same results. I think I can now leave by the end of the week."

With his sister out of serious danger Father Eymard returned to Paris to take up the work he had left behind and which awaited his attention.

BEYOND FRANCE

Now that the Jerusalem foundation was definitively out of the question he attended to a long-standing request to establish a community in Brussels. He had been in Belgium a number of times on preaching missions and it was during those visits that he had been approached by a wealthy woman, Ms. de Meeus, who was eager to have Eymard's Congregation in Brussels. He met her in October of 1865 at a friend's chateau at Ostreignie while he was recovering from a bout of cholera which was ravaging Paris at the time. Their meeting ended with an agreement that a chapel and some adjacent apartments would be made available to the Blessed Sacrament Community. With the archbishop's blessing the first foundation outside of France opened in Brussels on February 2, 1866, on the feast of the Presentation of Our Lord.

On the 6th of that month he wrote to Fr. De Cuers,

"I've been terribly busy, but here's a bit of news.… The Belgians are cold.… Our big fight was over the Roman liturgy and having them put aside their Belgian anti-liturgical practices for the pure Roman.

"Benediction of the Blessed Sacrament has been scheduled for three o'clock because the other churches have it at four and we don't want to provoke the neighboring parish priest if we have it at the same time as he does. We are obliged to drink beer because wine is so expensive here. Luckily Fr. Champion has sent us some Mass wine from his village. Our finances are very meager… but I refuse to ask anything of Ms. Meeus or from anyone else. Up to now we haven't been wanting for anything. But I do have a bill for bedclothes and for chairs;

could you send me the money you have put aside…?

"I received a letter from Bro. Francis asking for the money he had when he joined us in order to return to his mother before she dies…. I have no idea how much he gave, but it must be written down in Paris. I don't have any papers with me here.

"See if it's possible to have him wait till I get back to Paris. The awkward thing is that we don't have a Brother to replace him in the kitchen in Marseilles. It just goes to illustrate the need for each Brother to know how to cook in case of necessity; I'm going to do something about that here and in Paris. One day we were left in the lurch; it was a feast day and I had to do the cooking myself because Brother Francis had a terrible migraine attack."

Ten days later he wrote to Fr. Chanuet, the novice master, along the same lines,

"Thank you for the 200 francs; however, it left me a bit uneasy to know that you took it from your daily revenue. As soon as I get something I'll send it to you.… When Brother Francis gets his migraines we all become cooks with myself in the lead.… We carry on as if we were twenty, each brother serves two Masses, and what I admire and praise is that no one says a word or shows any sign of being over-burdened. They are genuine adorers out of love! We don't see anyone because we are always with the Lord. We have no garden, no wine, no heat, no marmalade; well, in any case we are happier than all of you because Our Lord has doubled the rations of grace."

These letters reveal the kinds of mundane, ordinary concerns Father Eymard had to deal with: financial matters; personnel problems; household chores. Nothing extraordinary, yet like a juggler at the end of a long and tiring performance he could not always manage to keep everything perfectly synchronized. He at times felt overwhelmed and unable to control the barrage of things coming at him all at once. He described the feeling to Mother Marguerite, "I do what people have to do when it rains and they have no umbrella; let the rain fall and get soaked." He did get soaked and he very nearly wrecked his health in the process. As much as he desired to suffer the hardships of establishing this new foundation, with all of its privations, his body could not withstand the strain. He fell gravely ill with shingles and a high fever.

"I'm still suffering," he wrote on March 1st, "I do not know what ails me, whether or not it's the measles. I've been without energy for some time.... the blotches come and go."

But a short while later to Fr. Chanuet he said,

"Don't worry about me. I've resumed my Eucharistic service. I no longer feel the fever. The shingles are going away. I didn't know why my shoulders were hurting at nighttime, nor why I had a pain by my heart.... On Friday when the doctor came I noticed I had these large pimples. I did what he said; he gave me a purgative which left me weak.... They frightened me with talk of measles and smallpox, but neither occurred. Last evening I preached, so you can see that my condition is improving.... I'm sending you a few hundred francs which we have collected here for candle wax."

Feeling himself gaining energy he resumed his duties but he suffered a relapse which left him bedridden and, at one point, very close to death with an extremely high fever. But a sudden eruption of the blisters lowered the fever and from then onward the illness took its normal course and he recovered.

Some time later he sent a letter to Fr. De Cuers, "I thought of calling for you before I got worse so as to bid you farewell.... I had asked God to let me die...." He realized how close to death he had actually come, "I want to tell you that I was sick and that I am still suffering.... Last Saturday I saw death close at hand.... I came to understand that we have only one refuge and that's the inexhaustible mercy of God and the goodness of Our Lord." But to someone else he explained, "The good God did not want me. He is letting me remain to do a little penance, so that I will not have long to stay in purgatory."

During the rest of the year, when he wasn't handling community matters, he was preaching or giving retreats, his favorite apostolates. At the end of April he was out preaching in the city of Ghent to a group called "Women of Adoration." The next month, having returned from Belgium, he preached at the Carmel of Bergerac; in July he preached a retreat at Mauron; in September he gave a retreat at Angers; then he went to Nemours to preach a retreat after making his final pilgrimage to the shrines of Our Lady of La Salette and Laus. In between these preaching assignments he searched the area close to Paris for an appropriate location and property to house a novitiate. He felt that the house of Paris had become too distracting to provide a proper formation and the number of novices was such that their presence was becoming a burden to the rest of the community. After many disappointments, he found a property at St. Maurice a short distance by train from Paris.

He broke the news about the purchase to Fr. De Cuers,

in June, "I'm writing to let you and the fathers and brothers of the community know the news that we have bought a house with its courtyard just two hours outside of Paris on the train line to Orleans.... This is really a stroke of divine Providence because we have all we need now for a novitiate and later for a house of solitude: 5.75 acres of enclosed land, a building in good condition which in time can accommodate 25 rooms, and a suitable chapel. The property was sold to the tribunal... for 77,000 francs. Our good and always devoted Fr. Chanuet will pick up the cost, at least most of it."

The house was not immediately ready for occupancy owing to a number of alterations and repairs that had to be done. Father Eymard, impatient to have the opening for Christmas, set out for St. Maurice and helped to get it ready. Two hours before midnight on Christmas eve he was still hammering parts of the altar in place. At midnight all was ready and he celebrated Mass with fourteen novices. This novitiate functioned at St. Maurice, except for a brief interval during the war of 1870, until the expulsion of all religious from France in 1880 when the property had to be sold to provide funds to set up a new novitiate in Brussels.

During this period he also took interest in setting up a project with Fr. Dhé, from the diocese of Paris, to work for the rehabilitation of priests. In a letter to Fr. Dhé he recalled how as far back as 1855 he had proposed such a scheme to the Holy Father who had responded favorably to the idea: "This notion is from God. I'm convinced that the Church needs this help. It must be done quickly." Father Eymard urged Fr. Dhé not to get discouraged by the possible difficulties involved but simply to trust in God's grace. He then attached a copy of a petition to the Pope which stated in part that he and Fr. Dhé had "devised a plan to dedicate ourselves to the task of rehabilitating [...] unfortunate priests." This project was left unrealized.

THE YEAR 1867

The new year brought him no respite from the cares of governing a new Congregation. Despite his demanding schedule he found time to continue his First Communion apostolate and, in addition, he assumed the teaching of classes to three young religious studying theology at the community. He was not spared the concerns and demands of community life. He wrote, in the early part of January, to Fr. De Cuers saying that some people were sick and that poor Bro. E. had not been able to correct his drinking habit and was obliged to leave the community. A few days later he wrote again to De Cuers,

> "I haven't been able to send you the additional priest you asked for, because I have none. Fr. Champion has made the same request and I told him the same thing. In a month and a half Bro. C. will be ordained... be a little more patient." He continued, "As far as your position as Superior, I wish you would continue; however, if this responsibility increases your suffering and keeps you from having peace of mind, I wouldn't want to insist. In that case I would relieve you.... Pray for me, for I barely have time to breathe."

By early spring he was again out looking for a new house in Paris. The community had recently been notified to vacate the property at Faubourg Saint-Jacques to make room for a street expansion project. A building was found at 112 Boulevard Montparnasse, an abandoned boarding house. Not having the funds to buy it he rented it until the money from the sale of the Saint Jacques property became available. The renovations of the new building had hardly begun when the demolition crews arrived. They moved in a hurry.

A few evenings later Father Eymard told Bro. Albert, "Take a basket and we will go fetch our poor cat. We forgot it and he surely must be starving." They found it amidst the debris of the Congregation's first motherhouse.

About this time, after extensive bargaining and a three month delay the bishop of Angers finally authorized Eymard to build a new church for their use in his diocese. The bishop had previously denied the Congregation the possibility of using an appropriately renovated theater and forced them to tear it down at considerable expense. Any excitement at the prospect of opening a new church in Angers was short lived because the community could not raise the capital for its construction. Father Eymard had hoped to cover the expenses by drawing on money he had invested in the publishing house of the Paris archdiocese only to discover that the firm was bankrupt. He wrote to the Superior of the Angers community explaining that the archdiocesan publishing firm, Leclerc, had collapsed,

> "A catastrophe has befallen us: the Leclerc failure; we had 67,000 francs there, and I was counting on this money for you. What an ordeal! It has paralyzed my pen as well as my joy.... As you can see misfortunes are rarely missing."

The bankruptcy disaster had upset him a great deal and had also thrown the financial security of the Congregation into disarray. He barely had time to assess the impact of this loss when he got a distressing letter from Marseilles. The bank there was demanding full payment of a loan which had been made for the purchase of the Marseilles property. Interest had been paid for eight years and now the bank was requiring full payment of the capital. These pressing and less than encouraging financial matters were demanding more and more of

Father Eymard's attention: "Angers is going to cost us a lot, Paris still has nothing, St. Maurice has yet to be paid up," is how he described the situation to the Superior of Marseilles.

There was also the question of the Nemours fiasco. The foundation of the Nemours community of the Sisters had been established on shifting sand from the start and soon developed into a long, bitter, and complicated saga which resulted in closing the community. The affair had serious consequences which left Eymard's competence discredited in the eyes of a number of bishops and his reputation, among his own senior religious, in shambles. Some of these financial entanglements resulted in court cases, and although each one of them was eventually satisfactorily settled, the stress began to drain his psychic energy.

The severest blow, however, came to him from Fr. De Cuers who, in the summer of 1867, once again decided to quit the Congregation. De Cuers wished to establish a "house of solitude" where there would be no apostolic ministry. His idea was to organize a contemplative community based on a monastic model of religious life. Father Eymard authorized him to follow this attraction as a personal venture; but Eymard refused to commit the Congregation to this approach. With three companions Fr. De Cuers began his experiment at Roquefavour, a wild and deserted place. They lived poorly, often with little to eat and with no financial means of support. Eventually the small group dispersed and Fr. De Cuers returned to the Congregation as he had done before but this time the founder would no longer be there to welcome him. Father Eymard visited him in January of 1868 never to see him again.

At the close of 1867 Father Eymard's single consolation, after a very stressful year, was the establishment of another community in Brussels which was intended to become a house for theological studies.

THE YEAR 1868

At the beginning of the new year Father Eymard was ill with influenza and running a high fever. No sooner had he recovered than he was again on the road. On January 4 he preached a retreat to the Marseilles community and visited Fr. De Cuers at Roquefavour. He complained of migraines throughout his stay in the south of France. He returned to Paris after spending a few days at La Mure. In mid-March he was in Angers where he preached twice a day, even though his legs could hardly support him. By the end of that month he was preaching another retreat, this time in Ghent in Belgium. Finally he took some time for himself and made a retreat at the novitiate of St. Maurice. His retreat notes reveal a soul in anguish as he reviews significant moments of his life:

"The state of my soul, now for three years so distressed, so sad, so desolate."

"Our Lord has called me to His Eucharistic service in spite of my unworthiness. He has chosen me to work for His Society in spite of my incompetence and my poor health. He has led me from death to the life of the Society."

"Death to the Society of Mary, so painful; death at the reception by the Archbishop of Paris after 13 agonizing days; death to self when deserted, left all alone; death in Paris when the Cardinal was minded to get rid of us; death from my subjects; death at Rome on the occasion of the Decree. The most distressing death of all (separation from my first companion); death from the loss of esteem of Bishops because of Nemours; loss of esteem of my own brethren because of...."

"My spiritual life is weak, sickly, dried up in me,
and has been so for a long time."

"When trials arose from without or from within,
a quarter of an hour before the Blessed Sacrament
used to strengthen and calm me, but today hours
leave me desolate."

He made his own the prayers found in Sacred Scripture.
There his soul was revealed and nourished.

"My innermost heart longs for God. *De profundis
clamavi* (out of the depths I cry). Psalm 130:1."

"My strength is dried up like a potsherd. Psalm
22:15."

"Blessed be God because he has not rejected my
prayer or removed his steadfast love from me.
Psalm 66:20."

For the rest of the month of May he was busy giving a
retreat to the Brothers of St. Vincent de Paul in Paris; preaching of Forty Hours devotions; and giving a final sermon begging for contributions for his privileged apostolate, "I
preached at Our Lady of Victories on behalf of the First Communion project. Collection: 450 francs." In June he returned
to Angers to lay the cornerstone of the new church.

This whirlwind of activity caught up with him.

On July 17 he left for Vichy, on the doctor's orders, for
an extended period of rest. Dating from Roman times, the spa
at Vichy was renowned for its water treatment for digestive
and liver ailments. He decided to meet Marguerite Guillot
there since she was seriously ill herself and in need of treatment. Some days before he had suffered a severe attack which

left his left arm almost completely paralyzed and two fingers on that hand considerably swollen.

He wrote to his sisters from Vichy, "I hope to see you by the end of the week. I came here to see Mother Guillot and some other people that I know. I must get to Lyons and from there I'll go to La Mure and to Our Lady of La Salette… I am so happy that I'll be able to see you, dear sisters; I wasn't expecting this favor from God because I have so many things waiting for me in Paris." This letter was dated July 19 and it was to be his last to his sisters.

Although he was suffering from rheumatic gout and sciatica there was nothing in his correspondence to his own religious which betrayed the likelihood of a very serious illness, even though in February he was laid up because of chest pains. His letter from Vichy to Fr. Stafford, a young priest in the Paris community, intimates nothing unusual,

> "I am here but the doctor does not want me to take the waters for my rheumatic gout but simply to breathe the mountain air…. I noticed from Fr. A's last letter that he is still not well. The best thing is to send him to Paris. It would be a shame if he were to break down. (…) Adieu, pray for me. I'm going to try to make my retreat at O.L. of Laus, my shrine of grace, if my rheumatism gives me a little respite. P.S. M. Guillot is here in great pain and had to stop taking treatments. She is very sick. The Gourd ladies are here too."

To his own religious confreres everything appeared to be business as usual. However, in his correspondence to his close and longtime lay friends he was quite frank and honest about his condition. In March he had written to a friend,

"I thought my time was up. But God did not think
I was ready. It's true; so many mistakes to make up,
so many things to do well!" "

His spiritual state matched his ailing physical condition.
He wrote in April to another friend,

"Pray for me, my dear, I need it so much. Sadness
is seeping into my soul with its desolation. Fortunately, it doesn't show."

At Vichy on Monday, July 20, he celebrated Mother
Marguerite's feast day with a meal at the Hotel Barre in the
company of Mrs. Gourd and her daughter, Stéphanie, both
long time benefactors. Later, recalling the event, Mother Marguerite remarked that he had remained very quiet throughout the meal and at two o'clock he bid them adieu, "I do not
want to fall sick here, it is time for me to go." With those parting words he left them.

Photo of Fr. Eymard

Calvary in La Mure

CHAPTER NINE

A Journey's End

"It is time for me to go."

FINAL DAYS

After spending the night in a hotel near the station in Lyons, Father Eymard took an early train to Grenoble. He left without eating breakfast because he intended to celebrate Mass upon his arrival at the chapel of the La Salette Fathers. Luckily, as he left the Grenoble station he met an old friend, Fr. Bard a diocesan priest, who walked with him to the chapel after making arrangements for a place on the coach to La Mure. With the La Salette superior in attendance he celebrated Mass with difficulty and was then persuaded to rest before catching the coach to La Mure. He was given some Chartreuse to drink before departing to strengthen him for the journey. He left the chapel around one thirty.

His friend accompanied him part of the way until he reached his own parish and then bid him farewell while instructing the coach driver to handle the horses carefully so as not to increase Father Eymard's discomfort and thereby aggravate his weakened condition.

The coach covered the grueling 30 kilometers during the

hottest part of the day. July can be unbearably hot. When Father Eymard arrived in the early evening he was physically drained from the five to six hour coach ride and suffering from heat exhaustion. His sisters attested that he came off the coach without a word and walked ahead of them to the house with his coat and umbrella over his arm. He climbed the stairs to his room and indicated that he wished to write something down. Of what he scribbled only the date and his signature were legible.

The following day revealed the true nature of his illness. That morning when his sister came to greet him he was unable to speak. His mouth was completely distorted. He had suffered a stroke thus leaving him partially paralyzed and incapable of writing or speaking. His condition remained unchanged for the next five days. On Monday, July 27, he sat up to drink some broth. The following days, however, saw no improvement; his breathing became more and more labored and he grew weaker as the days passed. On Friday he spent a very difficult night. In the morning Mass was celebrated in his room and he received Holy Communion. Around noon everyone gathered to say the prayers for the dying. Father Eymard followed the prayers but was unable to form the responses. Around two thirty his head slipped quietly to the side and he died peacefully. It was the feast of St. Peter in Chains, his patron. He was 57 years old.

As soon as they heard that he was dead the people of La Mure came running to see "Father Julian", as he was still known in his village, to join in the prayers for the dead and to touch his body with their rosaries and holy objects. The procession of pilgrims lasted well into the night.

The next day, Sunday, the doctor suggested that because of the suffocating heat in the upstairs room the body be brought downstairs. The body was dressed in a white alb and stole and at five o'clock about a dozen priests carried the body down the same streets he had run through as a child. After reciting Vespers in the church the priests transferred the body to the cemetery where the entire population of La Mure had gathered to bid adieu to "our saint" as they repeatedly described him. He was buried near the parish church where he remained until his Religious Congregation claimed the body and moved it to Paris.

Journeying
Today

"The point of departure is the Cenacle."

Peter Julian Eymard was a driven man. Although his life was short, the journey back to La Mure from his childhood days when he ran the streets ringing the bell to announce the morning Mass proved to be a long and arduous journey.

His whole life was a series of ventures each one more demanding than the last, each one requiring greater sacrifices, but each progressively leading to a richer understanding of his Eucharistic vocation. Little by little he realized the power of the Eucharist for Christian life. Every stage of his life seemed to lead him closer to this goal. Even though he died before fully codifying his vision he, nevertheless, laid a solid foundation upon which to build. His life and deeds spoke louder about this than the few words he left behind.

> "I feel that every road by which I traveled through the goodness of God was but a preparation for this wonderful and holy vocation; nor do I cease thanking God for having been with the Marists and to have been a parish priest and a curate."

Father Eymard was clear about the purpose of his new Congregation and that is why he was always reluctant to consider joining other religious communities who espoused a limited view of the Eucharist. It was the reason for which he opposed a strictly contemplative orientation in his Congregation. His petition to Pope Pius IX in August of 1855 was unequivocal:

> "The Society of the Blessed Sacrament would not confine itself to the mission of prayer and contemplation. It would in an apostolic way devote itself to the salvation of souls by employing every means inspired by prudent, enlightened zeal and the divine charity of Jesus Christ."

On December 15, 1867, six months before he died, Father Eymard addressed his community in Paris about the apostolic preference of the Blessed Sacrament Society:

> "The Society has two special works of zeal for the moment. They have been approved in the Decree of Approbation of the Society: the First Communion of poor children and the work for the sanctification of priests."

His vision of the Eucharist was remarkably comprehensive for the times in which he lived. It was a period in the Church's history when the Eucharist was understood, especially according to popular devotion in France, as Jesus imprisoned in the tabernacle who needed to be placed on His rightful throne to receive the homage and reparation of the faithful for the sins of an evil society. In France this need to elevate the Sacred Host upon a royal throne carried political overtones; the monarchy with its privileges had been rejected

by the Revolution, but a significant residue of royalist senti-
ment still remained vivid in the Catholic imagination. Eymard
who started from this position came to see, however, that "this
throne must first be erected in souls.... The real temple, the
true tabernacle, the throne of the King is the human soul."

There is no doubt that, in a sense, Father Eymard was inspired in part by the Eucharistic movements which were then
popular. But his graces and spiritual insights allowed him to
see more profoundly, though obviously not completely, some
of the implications of the Eucharist for Christian living. A
fuller development of Eucharistic spirituality, however, ma-
tured only a hundred years later at the Second Vatican Council.

One of the finest expressions of Father Eymard's final
thought was expressed in the following letter,

"The goal which we give ourselves in our little community is to honor Our Lord Jesus Christ in the
Blessed Sacrament in accordance with the purpose
of the sacrifice; namely, to offer [to God] adoration,
thanksgiving, reparation, and petitions, in other
words, a perpetual mission of prayer. We consider
the sacrament in its fullness. That's the reason for
which I was unwilling to go merely with reparation
[...] and a life exclusively contemplative. For us, we
not only want to adore, serve and love Jesus in the
Eucharist, but especially to make Him known,
adored, served, and loved by every heart."

For historical reasons, however, the most significant being his own untimely death, his two Congregations took on a
very contemplative and "cloistered" or monastic orientation
which lasted until recent times. Nevertheless, with the renewal
of religious life called for by the Church, Father Eymard's

spiritual disciples were able to renew their understanding of the founder's charism.

Father Eymard could not possibly have foreseen all the implications which contemporary theology has been able to offer the Church. He indefatigably lived his own life, with the graces granted to him by God, between the prie-dieu, the pulpit, and the people, especially the poor. The Eucharist for him was ever new because it was the source of the life of the Church and her richest achievement.

The Eucharist is to be shared as nourishment as well as adored. Father Eymard's own very active apostolic life offers a convincing model and a lasting witness to his spiritual legacy. As essential as was his prayer for his interior life, so was the apostolate the center of his priestly life. If his prayer was the heat of the fire, his apostolate was its flame. In March 1865 he was to write, "But shouldn't we have both contemplatives and apostles in the Society, both adorers and firebrands, since our Lord wants *this Eucharistic fire to set the world ablaze*? Who better than religious of the Blessed Sacrament can and should spread it everywhere and make our Lord known, loved, and adored everywhere."

The Eucharistic fire of which he spoke truly consumed him. Many years after his death people recalled vividly their encounter with him. Father A. Leclerc, Superior General of the Vincentians, gave this testimony in 1902:

"I said I met the Servant of God and heard him preach a triduum in our chapel of Notre Dame of Grace. Upon seeing him and hearing his sermons I experienced such a deep impression that it remains with me today even as I felt it on the first day. What first struck me was his ascetic bearing. He had a look of fire! It radiated in an ecstatic way from his face when his eyes were raised towards the Blessed Sacrament either in prayer or during his preaching. The feeling which his words produced in me were such that I have never felt anything similar in my life. I have heard some important people talk on the Eucharist, like Bishop de Ségur, one of the apostles of the Eucharist; but Father Eymard's style and power were totally different. He spoke simply, without any affectation; he adapted himself to his listeners. His words flowed like streams of light and fire. It was like a new revelation of the Eucharist for his listeners."

Today that fire, with its heat and its flame, continues to glow worldwide as the sons and daughters of Saint Peter Julian Eymard continue his mission by providing Christians with a Eucharistic spirituality. It is a spirituality, in the spirit of Saint Peter Julian Eymard, that centers a person's religious search in the Eucharist. The Eucharist is food for our journey; it is the bread broken for the life of the world and calls for justice and unity; it is the shared meal which builds the body of Christ, the Church. The Eucharist is the Bread of Life, it is the Lord's Supper where each one is summoned to wash the feet of others in a life of adoration and service. The Eucharist is the heart of discipleship.

Saint Peter Julian Eymard clearly saw the Eucharist as a powerful force for the renewal of Church and society.

Rule of Life of the
Congregation of the Blessed Sacrament

St. Peter Julian Eymard

Selections from
Saint Peter Julian Eymard

"Love is contemplative by nature.... Eucharistic contemplation is more active than passive; it consists in the soul giving itself unreservedly to God propelled by God's continually new and sweet goodness, and by the ever increasing flame of his love."

"Every religious group has its own way of praying.... We, too, must have our own method of praying.... We have adopted that of the Church in the Holy Sacrifice; that should suffice for us."

"At Mass, Jesus Christ offers himself to his Father, *adoring* him, *thanking* him, offering *reparation* to him, and *petitioning* him on behalf of the Church, of everyone, and of unfortunate sinners."

"Let us unite ourselves to [the prayer] of Our Lord; let us pray as He does with the four *attitudes* expressed at the Eucharist; this manner of praying sums up our worship."

"The Holy Spirit prays in us and for us. I could give you methods and rules for prayer; only the Holy Spirit can give you fervor and joy."

"The best method of all is the one fired by love."

"It is very helpful to pray according to the Spirit of the Church and to do so in harmony with the liturgical feasts."

RELIGIOUS LIFE

"Religious Life in Religious Orders is an end in itself; for us it is merely a means leading to greater things, to service of the Master.... [R]eligious life is simply the road leading to a Eucharistic life."

PRIESTS

"I want priests. Yes, my mission is to priests. It's my principal apostolate."

"I would give up everything for the sake of priests."

CHRISTIAN LIFE — HOLINESS

"Live one day at a time.... In fact, there is an important rule for holiness which is steadfast, true and always fruitful, it is: God's Will for us. In the Will of God, ever present and personal, we discover the 'grace of the moment' which leads to holiness. This grace comes at each moment and with every activity. When the moment passes and the activity is spent, so also the grace."

"Become a Saint! It's time; and to be a great saint you must be a person of prayer and generosity. It's essential that you want it and pursue it."

"The disciple of Jesus Christ can attain perfection in two ways. The first is according to the law of 'duty' which is long and difficult and few succeed. The second is shorter and more noble; it is the way of 'love.'"

"Society is dying because it has lost its center of truth and charity. Everyone is isolated and turned inward, wanting to be self-sufficient. A complete breakdown is imminent. But Society will come alive again when everyone gathers around Emmanuel. Relations will be re-established quite naturally around a common truth. Bonds of true and tried friendships will again be renewed through the power of shared love. It will mark the return of the lovely days in the Cenacle."

CENACLE

"I am convinced that I could satisfy the piety of Christians by simply exposing them to the Cenacle."

"Let us enter the Cenacle, the first church of the new law. This is where the Word Incarnate built his mystical mansion and supports it with the columns of the seven sacraments. This is where he sets his table for his disciples to eat with him."

"Our Lord begins from the Cenacle.... The evangelist says that He set out after having eaten. He had supper with them; the friend who shares, for the last time, his friend's bread. It is a meal of trust and love. We must set out from the Cenacle."

"The point of departure is the Cenacle. Why not Calvary or the crib? His point of departure is the Cenacle. There he loved and was loved. Jesus Christ renews the supper and repeats his testimony of love.... No one leaves a friend without a farewell meal. By sharing his bread he gave his life."

DEATH

"As the years advance, the weaker we get. It's like dying in stages. We have to accept it. But, fortunately, the heart never grows old; on the contrary, it gets younger by absorbing everything that the other faculties lose."

HOLY COMMUNION

"What name does Jesus give Himself? *Ego sum panis vitae.* I am the bread of life. Bread fulfills three needs: it feeds, it fortifies, it gratifies… basically, it nourishes."

"In your prayer seek rather to be nourished by God rather than to purify and to humble yourself."

"You take Communion to become holy, not because you already are."

"The Eucharist is the life of the people. The Eucharist provides them with a center for their lives. Everyone can gather without the barriers of race or language…. The Eucharist gives them a law to live by, the law of love of which it is the source; it creates a bond among them, one Christian family. They all eat the same bread; everyone is a guest of Jesus Christ who fashions a spiritual bond among them."

"And you especially, my sisters, what gives you respect within Christianity where elsewhere you are nothing more than slaves and objects in the hands of men? It is at Communion where you have the same rights as men. Communion honors your bodies and renders them participants of the Word made flesh…. You can approach the holy table without your husbands' permission. You have that right from God to sit at the celestial banquet."

THE POOR

"Tomorrow begins the retreat for the little ragpickers. God gave us the gift of the ultimate work of charity. They are the dregs of society. We teach them about God and about themselves.... What a ministry! I would not trade it for worthier causes. They are the little princes of the Eucharist whom we have sought out of the gutter."

LOVE

"In his love God created me. From all eternity he loved me within himself... then, in time, he created my soul out of the breath of his love; he created it in his image and likeness as the fruit of his love."

"Jesus loved me first, even when I didn't love him... Jesus loves me personally as if I were the only one on earth... with a tender love, a generous love, an unconditional love, a passionate love."

"We are getting older and there is still a long road ahead. We must take a short cut; and that is the road of love which gives without counting the cost."

"Strength springs from love; so love well. Love is the child of prayer; be a prayerful person. Your prayer, however, must be your own, loving and attentive, tasting God and being fed by him."

JESUS

"...go now, a little more by yourself, to be with Jesus in the desert where he whispers softly the secrets of the heart."

"Best of all, what is most nourishing and life giving is the spirit of Jesus in us; it is to be free and to live in him and for him."

"Jesus is mother. After giving you birth, he wanted to nurse you, to nurture you, to see you grow up and to guide you.... Our Lord's love is personal. [In Communion] it is for you that he comes."

"Jesus is the father who sets the family table. Through Jesus' paternity Christian brotherhood was promulgated at the Supper.... At the holy table all are children receiving the same food."

"Behold our strength and our joy: because of the Eucharist Christians can celebrate a feast where everyone, without jealousy or distinction, eats at the same holy table and drinks from the same heavenly cup. It is the happy feast of true brotherhood which continues forever.... Praise be Jesus Christ for leaving to his Spouse... his very self. It is for us to value it and to savor it."

VOCATIONS

"It is not for us to make vocations but to receive them from the divine Goodness. He who invites is the King, not the servants."

Saint Peter Julian searched for an answer to the religious ignorance and indifference of his time. He found it in the love of God manifested in a special way in the gift of Christ in the Eucharist. He was overwhelmed by this love and he proclaimed it to his contemporaries.

From the Rule of Life of the
Congregation of the Blessed Sacrament

Some Significant Dates in the Life of
Saint Peter Julian Eymard

1811, February 4	Born in La Mure, France
1834, July 20	Ordained for the diocese of Grenoble
1839, August	Enters the Marist novitiate in Lyons
1851, January 21	Special "grace" at O.L. of Fourviere
1856, May 13	Bishops in Paris confirm his charism
1863, May 8	Rome approves Eymard's Congregation
1865, July 6	Elected Superior General for life
1868, August 1	Dies at the age of 57 in La Mure
1925, July 12	Beatified by Pius XI
1962, December 9	Canonized by John XXIII

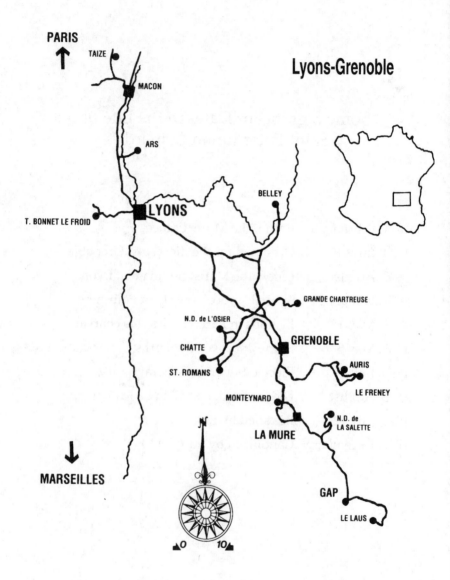

PARIS

TAIZE

MACON

ARS

BELLEY

Lyons-Grenoble

T. BONNET LE FROID

LYONS

GRANDE CHARTREUSE

N.D. de L'OSIER

GRENOBLE

CHATTE

AURIS

ST. ROMANS

LE FRENEY

MONTEYNARD

N.D. de
LA SALETTE

MARSEILLES

LA MURE

GAP

LE LAUS

0   10

PRAYER TO SAINT PETER JULIAN EYMARD
(LITURGICAL FEAST DAY — AUGUST 2)

Gracious God of our ancestors, you led Peter Julian Eymard, like Jacob in times past, on a journey of faith. Under the guidance of your gentle Spirit, Peter Julian discovered the gift of love in the Eucharist which your son Jesus offered for the hungers of humanity. Grant that we may celebrate this mystery worthily, adore it profoundly, and proclaim it prophetically for your greater glory. Amen.

Saint Peter Julian Eymard
Apostle of the Eucharist
Pray for us!

PRAYER TO OUR LADY OF THE BLESSED SACRAMENT
(LITURGICAL FEAST DAY — MAY 13)

Blessed are you, Mary,
exalted Daughter of Sion!
You are highly favored and full of grace,
for the Spirit of God descended upon you.
We magnify the Lord
and rejoice with you
for the gift of the Word made flesh,
our bread of life and cup of joy.
Our Lady of the Blessed Sacrament
our model of prayer in the Cenacle,
pray for us
that we may become what we receive,
the body of Christ your son.
Amen.
Our Lady of the Blessed Sacrament
Pray for us!

ST PAULS

This book was produced by St. Pauls/Alba House, the Society
of St. Paul, an international religious congregation of priests
and brothers dedicated to serving the Church through the communications media.

For information regarding this and associated ministries of the
Pauline Family of Congregations, write to the Vocation Direc-
tor, Society of St. Paul, P.O. Box 189, 9531 Akron-Canfield
Road, Canfield, Ohio 44406-0189. Phone (330) 702-0396; or
E-mail: spvocationoffice@aol.com or check our internet site,
www.albahouse.org